POWER GAMES:
WHY WINNERS WIN AND LOSERS LOSE

GERALD ALPER

POWER GAMES:
WHY WINNERS WIN AND LOSERS LOSE

GERALD ALPER

International Scholars Publications
San Francisco - London - Bethesda
1999

Copyright © 1999 by
Gerald Alper

International Scholars Publications
4720 Boston Way
Lanham, Maryland 20706

12 Hid's Copse Rd.
Cumnor Hill, Oxford OX2 9JJ

All rights reserved
Printed in the United States of America
British Library Cataloging in Publication Information Available

ISBN 978-1-57309-397-2 (pbk. : alk. ppr.)

To Anita

TABLE OF CONTENTS

PREFACE	x
CHAPTER ONE: Zero-Sum Relating...	1
THE INFORMER..	2
WRONGFULLY ACCUSED	7
BY THE BOOK	17
Counter Strategy..	25
THE VOICE OF EXPERIENCE...	27
"I USED TO BE THAT WAY"	30
RADIO RELATING...	31
"I HAVE A LOT OF PROBLEMS"..	35
A PERSON AND THEIR PSYCHIC PAIN SEEN AS AN	
INTERNAL OBJECT RELATION...................................	39
THE INFLUENCE OF PSYCHIC PAIN ON THE OTHER	39
"LET US PRAY"...	40
ONE-UPMANSHIP	53
NEGATIVE CLOSURE..	63
BEING IMPOSSIBLE..	66
BEING CRITICAL...	70
BEING ANXIOUS	73
GETTING IN THE LAST WORD	85
THE POWER OF CONTEMPT	86
Relationship To One's Contempt..	89
THE DENIAL OF A RELATIONSHIP	90
"I'M BORED"...	91
Using Boredom As A Ploy..	94
BEING CONDESCENDING	95
CHAPTER TWO: Who Wins, Who Loses...	101
DYNAMICS OF POWER GAMES.......................................	101
WORSHIPPING THE POWER GOD WITHIN...................	102
STRATEGIES FOR WINNING	103

DROPPING THE INFORMATION BOMB	103
PROVIDING USELESS INFORMATION	106
MUTING THE OTHER	110
THE DYNAMICS	112
DEADPAN	116
BEING THE STRAIGHT MAN	118
THE DENIAL OF MEANING	120
HOLDING ON	121
PAYBACK	122
DUELING NARCISSISTS	126
"JUST THE FACTS"	128
CHAPTER THREE: When Therapy Becomes a Power Struggle	133
"IT'S FOR YOUR OWN GOOD"	133
"I USED TO BE JUST LIKE YOU"	137
"I'M NOT GETTING ANY BETTER"	139
USING THE THERAPIST	141
CONCLUSION	145
REFERENCES	147
INDEX	149

Preface

The present work could be seen as a continuation and amalgam of two previous books: *Power Plays: Their Uses and Abuses in Human Relations* (Alper, 1998) in which I explore from a phenomenological standpoint the vicissitudes of power operations in everyday life and *Minding the Other's Mind: The Factor of Control in Contemporary Relationships* (Alper, 1997) in which I examine, psychodynamically, the devious ways by which people fall prey to external, and often internally imposed, manipulation.

A power transaction, as I define it, arises when there is a covert attempt to impose rules on the behavior of the other, rules, moreover, which, regardless of how they are rationalized—typically as being "for your own good" are clearly meant to benefit only one person (the antithesis, one might say, to the rationale underlying the multitude of bylaws, customs and mores comprising the social contract—that everyone supposedly shall be collectively better off).

The position that I take here vis-a-vis contemporary game theory is derived in good part from my essay, "The Theory of Games and Psychoanalysis" (Alper, 1993). It is to be located somewhere between the discrete behavioral series of moves seen in such classic games as "Prisoner's Dilemma" and the more psychodynamically oriented transactions portrayed memorably by Eric Berne in *Games People Play* (1964). This is because such psychodynamic patterns that emerge in the course of a psychoanalytic psychotherapy show neither the sequential behaviors of traditional game theorists nor the elegant convolutions of R.D. Laing's *Knots* (1970) or Berne's *Games People Play*.

As I see them, they are instead rough-hewn psychodynamic strategies unconsciously enacted primarily to spare the person the imagined angst that would be stirred up by anything remotely approximating, at that particular dynamic moment in time, an authentic encounter. Although the power games that follow can be characterological, they do not have to be: all people, even those rare individuals who are capable of ongoing intimacy, are forced at moments of frailty or interpersonal indecisiveness to play power games, and certainly the culture at large pervasively sponsors the enactment of opportunistic interpersonal strategies.

Power games in chapter one are introduced under the concept zero-sum relating—a transaction between two parties in which a gain for one side entails a roughly corresponding loss for the other side. In chapter two, the characteristics of power games and dynamics of strategies that are unconsciously perceived as conferring a winning advantage, are explored. In chapter three, games that are transacted covertly in the consulting room, between therapist and patient, are delineated. And in the conclusion, I present a brief overview of what I consider the most critical and durable issues that have been raised.

Once again, the people portrayed, howsoever briefly, are based on actual patients I have known and worked with, and are presented as they were originally seen by me through the prism of psychoanalytic psychotherapy. While the names, of course, have been changed and circumstantial details have occasionally been altered in order not to betray the confidentiality to which they are entitled, the incidents that are described, and, especially, the psychological dynamics which are depicted, are as true as I can make them.

CHAPTER ONE

Zero-Sum Relating

In retrospect, what I have variously termed zero-sum relating, strategic relating, addictive relating and behavioral puppetry—when considered as concepts—bear a family resemblance.

If so, what are the preconditions for the emergence of this kind of non-intimate engagement?

Perhaps foremost is a perception of a negative differentiation between self and other regarding core interests. A need for opportunistic strategizing grows naturally out of a feeling of distance, alienation and, especially, imagined or perceived conflicts. And although two people locked in a symbiotic union will sometimes anxiously resort to strategy to gain satisfaction for dependent needs that are not being met, they prefer to cling, when they can, to a fantasy of unrestricted, magical cooperation.

By contrast, the desire for or belief that one requires leverage in one's dealings with the other can be a product of an anxious sense that time is running out, that a dubious resolution is about to be reached, that one is in danger of being short changed or frustrated unless one acts and intervenes in a state of affairs that does not seem to be advantageous to one's best interests (or, from a more optimistic perspective, that a rather exceptional opportunity for need-gratification is in the offing and needs only to be seized).

Power games characteristically are devoid of originality. They are built instead on familiarity, the awareness that one has experience in this sort of operation and has therefore acquired certain tricks of the trade that can be profitably employed. Their use implies that one trusts one's defenses and resources considerably more than the good will and nurturing intention of the other. It follows that their arrival is contingent upon a mistrust of the other. To participate in power operations is to enter a solipsistic world where the only assets are those which emanate from the self, where one has no choice but to live by one's wits. Unconsciously, such transactions promote a linear Darwinian perspective: an interpersonal field of action ruled by the principal of competition and the survival of the fittest; where there are only winners and losers, where doubt as to the outcome can provide a soap-opera-like suspense, but where the tantalizing prospect that a victory is at hand can convey a heady sense of one's boldness and strength.

To the power player relating is a game to be played and to be won. If success is to come from one's skill, and at the other's expense, it is necessary to learn the rules and the strategies that prevail—which always implies an abandonment or temporary suspension of one's investment in intimacy. There are literally thousands of such games played millions of times daily in America. What follows are everyday examples of some of the more prevalent and important ones. Clinical vignettes are interspersed or supplemented with a running commentary. And my hope is that their accumulated weight will make the theme of this book come convincingly to life.

THE INFORMER

Sidney was more proud of himself than perhaps I could ever remember him. For once, he was not going to take it on the chin. For once, he was going to make someone sorry for what they had done to him. And it was just a matter of time, as he had already set in motion the process by which a formal complaint is lodged.

The designated payback victim who had so infuriated Sidney—who had prompted him to become an informer for the first time in his life—was the organizer of the business seminar, an ordinary-looking, low-key, overweight woman, who had escaped his attention at first. It was only when this woman approached the podium and announced there was now only standing room available to the jam-packed conference room that he noticed her. Sidney could not help noticing her since he apparently was one of the standing room crowd, in spite of the fact he had preregistered months ago and had paid one hundred dollars for his ticket. But to his chagrin when he arrived about ten minutes past the scheduled start time, as was his wont, he discovered that seats were not only not reserved but were all taken.

Incensed, as it dawned on him that someone who had bought a standing room ticket must have swiped a seat that was meant for him, Sidney made a beeline for the organizer who was getting ready to announce the first scheduled speaker. Prepared to walk out of the seminar and demand a refund if he did not get a seat, he was surprised how unruffled, if slightly annoyed, this woman appeared to be upon being presented with his last minute ultimatum. "Then, I'll give you my chair," she calmly replied, quickly leaving the room and reappearing in less than a minute with a simple folding chair that she proceeded to set up at the far side of the room.

So, thinking the matter had been settled and pleased with himself for being so uncharacteristically forthright, Sidney switched his attention to the speaker who was inaugurating a panel discussion of strategies for finding a better job. Four hours later, when the lunchtime break had rolled around and his head was chock-full of novel schemes for prying himself free of his current job as an assistant manager in a travel agency, which he absolutely loathed, Sidney felt he had already received his money's worth. Yet, he could barely wait when he had finished his lunch to return to the seminar in the hope of garnering even more tools to jumpstart his non-existent career.

Upon reentering the conference room, Sidney was immediately irritated to find it no less jam-packed than before. As he began surveying the crowd, he realized that he was vaguely worried that he might experience a similar difficulty in locating an available seat. He was relieved when the organizer stepped to the podium to announce that everyone was to return to the same seats that they had been sitting in. Even when he caught sight of the slight, blond-haired man who now occupied his chair, he was not overly concerned. After all, he felt reinforced by what the woman had just said and, besides, hadn't he successfully asserted himself in the morning?

Nevertheless, he was aware of a small fluttering in his chest and quickening of his breathing—signs he associated in the past with stressful situations, especially moments of confrontation—as he neared the trespasser.

"Excuse me. You're sitting in my chair."

If anything, the blond-haired man seemed amused, rather than informed. Smirking, he pointedly glanced at his watch, which he lifted in the air for dramatic purposes: "You come ten minutes after the session is supposed to begin and ask for a chair?"

At once Sidney's resolve crumbled. Fearing he was about to be rendered speechless, he blurted, "I was sitting here all morning."

"You didn't leave anything on the chair."

"The woman said everyone should return to their seats."

"Then you'll have to bring someone over to settle this. I'm not giving you this chair."

Feeling infuriated, but momentarily beaten, Sidney retreated to the podium, where he managed to intercept the organizer who had already made some preliminary attempts to kick off the afternoon session.

"You remember me. You gave me your chair this morning. Look, it's happened again. That man over there stole my chair. He says I should bring someone over to settle this. You remember I was sitting over there, don't you?" Sidney pointed miserably in the direction of the blond-haired intruder.

"Put yourself in my shoes. What would you do? I have a seminar to run."

In the session Sidney sneered at the organizer's plea for empathy for behavior which to him was both despicable and personally humiliating. He was cognizant that he lacked the courage to do what he really wanted to do: wait until the seminar was over, corner the blond-haired man who had stolen his chair and then punch him in the center of his smirking face. Getting even with the overweight woman whom he had unrealistically counted on to rescue his wounded pride was clearly an alternative plan, but it would have to do. Sidney was far too agitated to let the slight go without trying to make somebody pay.

Much of the following day—after a relatively sleepless night in which he could not help tormenting himself by replaying the scene over and over in his mind--was spent in tracking the woman down, ascertaining the name of the supervisor to whom she was directly answerable, and finally composing a lengthy and well-argued, detailed letter of complaint.

In subsequent weeks, Sidney discussed just how meaningful it had been for him to officially report what he had considered grossly negligent behavior on the part of the organizer, and how he had become prone to frankly sadistic fantasies in which he would picture the dismay of the woman and the outrage of her supervisor upon receiving his damning letter.

As his therapist, I was privy to Sidney's susceptibility to feelings of humiliation when he felt he was unfavorably thrust into the public eye. He had on more than one occasion described the panic that would overtake him when he found himself boxed into a confrontational encounter that promised to be unpleasant. I could therefore appreciate the level of frustration and resentment that must have been experienced, that was required to drive Sidney to initiate a possibly serious confrontation by informing on the organizer. But I was also struck—especially given the current, politically correct emphasis on treating the reputation and social standing of the other as something almost sacred—with the intoxicating sense of power that can come with the realization that you are ready in some way to publicly impugn the character of the other.

To inform, therefore, typically feels like an act of daring assertiveness. In effect, the informer is defying some fundamental, if implicit social injunctions: "Don't make waves" ... "Don't create unnecessary enemies" ... "Don't let them know what you're really thinking" ... "Don't say or do anything you can't later conveniently retract" ... and "If in doubt, be nice". Because it plainly flies in the face of socially ingrained ideas of what civilized behavior is supposed to be, it seems dangerous. The person, by informing, locks himself into a profoundly antagonistic position vis-á-vis the other. By formally challenging their ability to perform a particular job, the informer commits himself to being a threat to the other's basic survival. Officially he chooses to embrace a destructively negative version of the other, akin to casting a public vote against them.

But what of the reaction of the other? She cannot help—when she is apprised of the gravity of the charge against her—feeling betrayed. Someone has gone over her head to ally himself with a higher authority for the express purpose of punishing and controlling her. Unconsciously this can only be taken as proof that the person has given up on any prospect of working out the impasse and opted to terminate the former relationship. Instead, in a seeming complete turnabout, the person has chosen to prosecute the relationship, which now is defined strictly in terms of malfunctioning or wrongdoing. The question becomes—not what possibilities are there for mutual benefit—but how successfully will the allegation of negligence be supported or refuted?

Someone who is thus officially called to accountability—even if fully conscious that she was in egregious bad form, in a foul mood which she acted out against an innocent customer who just happened to be in the wrong place at the wrong time—will characteristically feel unlucky, misunderstood and ganged up against. The customer, instead of granting her any slack for having a bad day or giving her a second chance to make reparation, is holding her to an absolute standard of accountability for what may well be an isolated mishap. From the standpoint of the one being called up on the carpet—who may in fact have handled the very same situation in the past many times without a single miscue or complaint—it will seem that the informer is laboring under a highly subjective and distorted version of what happened, and on the basis of an extremely improbable occurrence is making a wildly unjustified accusation (fueled by their narcissistic injury).

Inasmuch as this accusation, if sustained, will likely damage the reputation of the other, it can only seem heartless, self-centered and vindictive. The informer has caught someone with their worst side showing and pounced on it to thoroughly discredit them.

Holding the other to accountability in this fashion will have psychic resonance. It is, after all, only a public projection of the daily operation of our superego when it is being especially hard on us. In contrast, to the unspoken, comparatively fluid boundaries of ordinary, interpersonal interacting—wherein you are often allowed to somewhat transgress a particular boundary, provided you are willing to step back when necessary and make amends—a rule or regulation sets an arbitrary, narrow limit, which if crossed, is not tolerated or forgiven and becomes the basis for a label of wrongdoing that cannot be redressed by the transgressor, but must be settled by an external, higher authority. In other words, within the defined parameters under which there is hegemony of the regulation, there can be no mistakes. It is from such an absolutist climate—based on the unconscious dread that the reputation of the self could be ruined in the eyes of the superego by a single, serious mistake—that the power game of interpersonal informing can arise.

WRONGFULLY ACCUSED

The considerable psychic damage that can be the aftermath of being punitively held accountable, is perhaps best exemplified by the person who unexpectedly realizes he is being accused of a crime he did not commit.

In this regard I think especially of Darryl, a brilliant graduate student of philosophy, who—considering himself an unlucky loser when it came to personal relationships—was resigned to spending his spare time in the company of good books. To satisfy this craving Darryl had visited well over a hundred book stores in the borough of Manhattan alone, before settling on a small out-of-the-way place in the West Village that for some reason, and to his deep gratitude, stocked only the finest of high brow, esoteric books. In no time at all, Darryl became a fixture to the personnel of the store: endlessly browsing, hungrily scanning the new titles section for possible discoveries; striking up conversations with the book clerks whenever he could and invariably making a purchase, even when he could not afford to.

In the three years that I knew him, Darryl, who supported himself by working part time on graveyard shifts at an all night restaurant, must have bought thousands of dollars worth of books from this single store. As far as he was concerned, he was a special customer, a kindred spirit to the clerks who, in Darryl's mind, were also book lovers. He was therefore totally unprepared for the incident which he would subsequently describe as the most degrading in his life.

On this fateful Saturday afternoon Darryl, as was his custom, had dropped in on his beloved bookstore. He did not notice the two large electronically wired gates which had recently been installed about five feet from the front door. He did not pay any attention to the book he was carrying with him in plain view since he never went anywhere without something to read. He simply nodded to the gangly young woman at the cash register—an earnest student at the NYU film school, with whom he had perhaps had scores of casual conversations over the past few years—and proceeded to head for the new titles section.

But no sooner had he passed through the gates, than he was startled by a loud, angry ringing, which sounded like an alarm bell being set off. Instinctively Darryl slowed in his tracks, not wanting to believe, yet sensing that somehow he had been responsible for the disturbing noise. Remembering that he had once seen the book he was now carrying—*The Complete Short Stories of Franz Kafka*—in the store, he wondered if that possibly had anything to do with what had just happened. Not knowing why he was feeling uncomfortable and guilty, but thinking he should offer some kind of explanation, he approached the young woman at the cash register, who was strangely staring at him. Darryl placed the Kafka book squarely on the counter in a gesture of openness. "I brought this into the store. I don't know if that made the bell ring." He tried to look as though he were simply trying to find the answer to a puzzle.

Without a word, the woman stepped from behind the counter, took possession of the book and purposefully walked through the electronically wired gates. Almost immediately, there was a loud ringing. As though to replicate her findings, she retraced her steps three more times, in each instance eliciting the same wailing response.

By now, Darryl had begun to feel an incipient panic. Needing reassurance that he was not going to be blamed for something, Darryl added, "Why is it ringing?"

"It means the book was in the store."

As the implications of this statement began to sink in, Darryl was aware that he was beginning to take shorter and shorter breaths. It suddenly seemed important that he recollect just where he had purchased this book, and it came to him that he had discovered it lying on a street peddler's table that had been temporarily set up in front of the New York University library. But his heart sank as he reminded himself—as a native New Yorker and sophisticated book buyer he could not be ignorant of the possibility—that sometimes these books had originally been stolen.

"Why do you want to know if the book has been in the store?" He realized that it was a stupid question, but Darryl could not think of anything else to do, anything else to save face, except pretend that together they were investigating a moderately interesting, harmless, mechanical anomaly. He glanced warily at the woman, who, unable to look at him, had begun nervously to riffle the pages of the book. In a low voice, she responded, "It means it's been stolen."

The panic grew in Darryl. For a moment he had an impulse to reclaim his book—which now seemed tainted, potential evidence to be used against him—even if it meant snatching it out of her hands and fleeing the store. But why could he not look her in the eye, just tell her he had bought the book from a nearby street peddler and that if the book had indeed been stolen from the store, it surely was not, nay could not, have been him? And why, instead—unable to address her increasingly dark, accusing attitude—did he simply, softly, meekly say, "I'd like my book back."

"No, I need to keep this." Her courage growing with her indignation, she placed the book on a shelf beneath the counter and reached for a nearby phone. "Is Bill there?"

Terrified that he was about to be interrogated by the owner—a tall, dour man who periodically would stroll through the store, who once flattered Darryl by noting, "You must be one of our best customers, I see you all the time"—he was immensely relieved to learn that Bill would not be in until the following Monday evening.

As though the issue had now switched from the meaning of the ringing bell to the appropriate time for him and Bill to continue this discussion, Darryl—announcing that he would return on the same Monday—quickly left the store.

Immediately he returned to his apartment, his head buzzing with schemes for triumphantly clearing his good name. But once his panic had subsided, he faced the fact that he could not directly prove his innocence. The most he could do was to document his unquestionable and extraordinary love of good books and to that end he spent hours rummaging through his old tax records in search of possible sales receipts. To his delight, he was able to dig up about one thousand dollars' worth—testifying to an uncommon patronage of a single store over an unbroken period of three years—and bolstered by his receipts, the following Monday evening he telephoned the woman who had confiscated his Kafka book.

Recognizing her voice the moment she answered the telephone, Darryl, after pointedly reminding her of his scheduled appointment with Bill, indicated he had something he wanted to talk to her about.

Darryl could hear the indecision in her voice on the other end of the line, sense that she had been taken aback by the call. "I'll have to get back to you. Give me your number," she said slowly and then quickly hung up.

As he waited, he began to pace the room, rehearsing in his mind what he would say. He did not want to deal with Bill. His hope was that the presentation of one thousand dollars worth of sales receipts would carry such weight as to dispel any lingering doubts that he might be an actual book thief. The phone rang. To his dismay, it was not the woman, but Bill.

"Here's what we're going to do," he announced, after officially introducing himself as the proprietor himself. "You can come and pick up your book. But after that, I'm going to have to ask you not to come in the store anymore."

"Why? Because of the bell?" Darryl could barely speak.

As though responding to a technical question concerning the mechanics of theft detection, Bill started to expound: "Each book in the store is coded with magnetic whisper tapes. When a book is taken out of the store, the bell rings."

"But I brought the book into the store. Why do you mention the bell ringing? What does the bell ringing have to do with anything?" His voice rising, Darryl realized that he was becoming infuriated by the condescending manner in which the owner was treating him.

All of a sudden, however, Bill, apparently enraged himself by the show of resistance that Darryl was offering, began to scream, "IT MEANS THAT THE BOOK WAS STOLEN. IT MEANS YOU, IN EFFECT, OPENED UP MY WALLET AND TOOK MONEY OUT OF IT. AND THAT WAS A LOWLIFE THING TO DO."

And Darryl, as suddenly, as startlingly, especially to himself, at the top of his lungs, louder than he ever before had in his life, screamed, "FUCK YOU."

Of the various elements of shame and humiliation encapsulated in this experience, the most traumatic for Darryl had been the moment when he realized he was being accused of what for him was an unspeakable act. He likened that moment to an eerie sick feeling, an incipient panic which could not be expressed for fear it would be taken as a further indication of guilt: i.e., if you're honest you have nothing to fear.

To the extent, however, that someone, such as Darryl, feels compelled to pretend that he is unaffected, he feels dishonest and to that extent he may feel unconsciously somehow worthy of the accusation. Being accused can therefore mean that the entire interpersonal field of potentially infinite diversity and possibility has suddenly been shrunken to a blot or abyss of concrete, alleged turpitude. As though the issue has now, and seemingly forever more, become one of prosecution and defense, where everything that could matter will hinge on the determination of the degree of guilt or innocence. So that now there are no longer two selves, there is only the specter of a psychic or real crime which must be dealt with. Until such time, interrelating in any ordinary sense is not only to be put on hold, but is considered irrelevant. In its stead, the standards of highest morality, the honoring of traditional taboos, the punishment to be meted out to transgressors of the social order, are to command priority.

When someone is wrongfully accused, a deep-seated sense of guilt—the manifestation from a psychoanalytic point of view of their repressed, unacceptable impulses—is immediately triggered. It does not matter at an unconscious level that the person may be innocent, as Darryl was, of the particular charge that is being levied against him. What does matter is that the person invariably has much to be guilty about and has now been found out. Also interpersonally reinforcing the person's psychic sense of guilt is the palpable confidence of the accuser: i.e., since it significantly flies in the face of social conventions to seriously accuse another, one must be quite sure (analogous to the familiar public perception of someone who is charged with a crime—that they wouldn't be pointing their finger at them unless there was something to point at).

Not only everyday interrelating is suspended, however, time itself can seem frozen. As though a moment of truth has arrived, the gravity of which transcends the preoccupations of ordinary linear time. Instead, the soul or core of the self, one way or another, is to be revealed: by innocence shining through, or by a defensive covering up which bespeaks, in spite of itself, an undeniable guilt. Put another way, to levy an accusation is to create an instant rupture in the normally uneventful march of interpersonal time and the ensuing trial, whether legal or psychological, can be looked upon as an unconscious reparative attempt to abreact the traumatic affects that have been engendered.

For all of these reasons, in order to accuse another, it is necessary to psyche oneself up, to harden oneself considerably, to become far more inhuman than one customarily is—since to accuse someone of a moral or legal crime is to assert a position that is the radical antithesis of being nurturing and empathic—and to thereby identify with the grandiosity of being openly punitive and judgmental vis-á-vis a fellow human being. There is therefore a sense in which a person who is getting ready to accuse another is analogous to the military recruit in combat training: a concerted effort is made to eradicate the soft, empathic, identificatory links with the designated hostile other, who in turn is to be rigorously reduced to a monolithic, loathsome personification of his alleged inequity.

Not surprisingly, such a person will be subject to a considerable pressure and obligation to back up the accusation with objective evidence so as not to seem persecutory in an unfair or vicious way. Since, however, it is almost impossible to maintain such judge-like demeanor for very long, the accuser will often lapse into and settle for a distancing posture of moral repugnance, contemptuous skepticism and general scorn. Although obvious, it is overlooked that to accuse the other is to go beyond an interpersonal point of no return in which there can be no realistic possibility of dialogue, negotiation, or even debate. The plain fact that the person—analogous to the criminal prosecutor—cannot realistically withdraw a charge that has been made is terrifying to both parties because it means a door has been closed that is considered essential to the possibility of civilized social life: i.e., that someone who has committed an impropriety will almost always be given a chance to make amends. There is no such face-saving, however (in the sense used by Erving Goffman, 1967) for the one who stands accused.

In effect, to accuse someone is to place yourself in a superordinate position. To maintain this, however, it is necessary to establish an unequivocal moral superiority to the other; hence the posture of grandiosity. But this, of course, is difficult to uphold and what often happens after the shock wave of the initial public expression of accusation has worn off is a secondary phase—one of partial rapprochement. This is analogous to plea bargaining, in which there is an attempt—characterized by withdrawal and an aloof cynicism—to get along in a somewhat less confrontational style: a style, that is, wherein one waits to see if the other confesses guilt, shows signs of reparation, or presents some extenuating circumstances. All the while, however, there is a sense that the other has been permanently dispelled from the person's good graces after having clearly disgraced himself. At times, there may even be a note of condescending pity for someone who has just self-destructed (e.g., the owner of the bookstore announcing, "Here's what we're going to do ...").

As for the accused, it is almost impossible, as it was for Darryl, to avoid the instantaneous development of at least a situational paranoia. Such a person is typically confused in addition to being panicked. The experience we are describing is one that—for the ordinary individual, if it happens at all—occurs perhaps only a handful of times. When it does, it unconsciously represents the traumatic antithesis of the normal mechanism of social interaction, wherein someone, by consensual agreement, is characteristically bathed in a better light than they deserve (as described by Goffman, 1967): that is, here the person is of necessity presumed guilty and the burden of proof is shifted to the other to reestablish, if they can, their innocence and trustworthy social standing.

For all of these reasons, after the initial paralyzing shock has subsided, anger sets in: the person senses, even if they believe their innocence can eventually be proven, that they have suffered a terrible narcissistic injury and that their reputation can never be the same. Trust, to the extent that it existed prior to the accusation, cannot be restored. The anger that is felt therefore is not just a needed adrenaline rush to motivate oneself to counter the charge, but expresses a wish to punish the accuser for daring to disturb the social peacefulness that had previously been maintained. At the same time the person has to decide whether to act upon the anger--a risky move that could easily backfire and provoke the accuser to retaliate by escalating his charges—or to rein it in and use it instead to covertly rally one's defenses. A related consideration is whether to act quickly so as to nip a potentially explosive situation in the bud, or to bide one's time before seriously responding in order to assess the state of the other's evidence (and thereby not prematurely tip off one's defense strategy).

The main fear in biding one's time, of course, is that the accuser, unless immediately satisfied she is mistaken, will sooner or later begin to tell other people, if only to relieve the burden of what she now thinks she knows (as was the case with the woman at the cash register and which precipitated Darryl's confrontation with the store owner). On the other hand, if the person does decide to act on his anger--something Darryl was unable to do until it was too late--the most effective counterattack will be to disdain the need to prove one's innocence, and to assert instead that the charge must be false since one cannot be the kind of person who would do such a thing. This comes to saying, in effect, that "since it is impossible I would do that, you must be seriously and infuriatingly out of touch with reality". It is often followed up by daring the other to indisputably prove their charge, thereby shifting the burden of proof while conveying the latent threat that they better be mindful of the penalty for libelous actions.

In short, this most aggressive of defensive strategies turns the tables by accusing the accuser of the crime of a libelous accusation. But it is also one of the most difficult to pull off because the person has to not only absorb but quickly overcome the initial and usually considerable narcissistic injury of being accused so as to mount the countercharge with a sufficient degree of conviction. Needless to say, ordinary social, not to speak of neurotic insecurities, especially guilt feelings associated with the act in question—as was the case with my patient and is usually the case—will tend to nullify this strategy.

A more moderate, secondary defense, therefore, will be to ignore the darker implications of guilt and moral turpitude—which from an interpersonal standpoint are what is most dynamically interesting—and act as though what is at stake is merely the resolution of some impersonal process or event (e.g., the bell going off) that happens to tangentially involve them. The suggestion is that whatever happened, there was no intention to commit a wrongdoing. A mistake at most, but not a crime, is admitted (e.g., the Nixon defense, "I'm not a crook", or the Jimmy Carter defense, for failure of the mission to rescue the American hostages in Iran, "I take full responsibility for what happened" (but not any blame). This can be attractive to both parties because it allows the situation to be remedied—making reparation for the damage done, returning goods alleged to be stolen—without having to deal explicitly with any suggested underlying immorality or criminality. It thereby converts a possible sociopathic or pathological interaction into a straightforward business or social impropriety, something that can be handled in a practical fashion. In so doing, it denies that an untraversable gulf, from the standpoint of interrelating, has just opened up.

Such defenses, however, are rarely utilized by someone, such as Darryl, who is caught off guard and wrongfully accused. It scarcely helps that you know you are innocent and may one day prove your innocence. What seems decisive is that the other could actually think so incredibly little of you. There is a need to believe that there are certain unspeakable acts—regardless of the evidence—of which no one would believe you were capable. In the unconscious, therefore, in addition to the denial of one's physical death, there is the denial of one's psychical death: that one could be symbolically annihilated by the malignant perception of the other. There is a certain point, therefore, when one feels sufficiently misunderstood and hated, when the experience begins to feel uncanny, as though one is really capable, so far as one's true self is concerned, of becoming invisible to the other. In other words, although it can be validating, in a negative sense, to be hated for the genuinely aggressive elements in one's self, it is eerie to be hated because one is perceived to be an almost totally alien being.

To be wrongfully accused—the other trying to force-feed a hideous anti-identity into you—can be tantamount to soul snatching. It is to be reminded—analogous to the person who sees their inbuilt denial of death beginning to crumble because of their growing identification with the dying processes of a loved one--that the denial of psychic annihilation is a similar illusion. And this can be a traumatic violation of one's sense of basic trust (Erikson, 1959) and an example instead of a sudden, chilling appearance of malign betrayal (the sense that something has happened that was not supposed to happen—Bollas, 1995).

Although, of course, to be accused of a crime one did not commit is a rare occurrence, its psychic analogue—to be misunderstood, misperceived and devalued to such a profound extent that one cannot recognize oneself—is an almost universal possibility that can be instantiated by the other at any moment. It is this freedom that each of us has to internally define the true self of whomever we encounter that can, if we choose, make even the shadow of our judgmental disapproval a potent power game.

BY THE BOOK

Of all my patients, none was more sensitive to the rebuff of being dealt with in a routinized, impersonal manner than Merle, an attractive, middle-aged school teacher who was trying to make sense of her new life as a recently divorced woman. Now that she was finally on her own, and living alone for the first time in her life in a simple, cheerless Queens apartment, she had plenty of time to think about all the people who, supposedly there for her, had really let her down: her former husband who had effectively deserted the marriage soon after it had begun for a series of meaningless but necessary affairs; her assortment of friends who were consistent in their praise for her qualities as a person, her oft-noted kindness and thoughtfulness, but never seemed to be available when it came to her needs; her mother, a reliably and mildly comforting presence, who could be counted on for a loyal, but mindless support; and her father, an unaffectionate, demanding, aggressively self-involved man, who died suddenly of a heart attack when Merle was in graduate school and is chiefly remembered by her as an irritably impatient, somewhat heartless figure who seemed devoid of interest in her.

In therapy it became clear that Merle traced the root of her overreaction to and dread of being discounted by others to her father's impregnable indifference.

Increasingly, sessions were filled with complaining narrations of suspected or perceived mistreatment from people she had encountered. She was particularly leery of sales personnel, shopkeepers, menial workers—"relating by the book" she called it—those who were occupationally compelled to put up a perfunctory front when dealing with the public.

Thus when the building super, a heavyset South American man built along the lines of a wrestler, who was here on a green card, was summoned to investigate the source of a leak from her bathroom ceiling, it was not the scope of his skills that preoccupied Merle. It was the lazy, sensual and almost sneering way he appeared to survey the range of her living space, as though curious as to whether someone else might be there, which in turn made Merle wonder why he would care. She would note how the security man in the lobby would perform his lifeless ritual of opening the door for her at the very last moment, when it could not be avoided, yet would immediately become animated when someone, anyone, supplied the latest or even tiniest tidbit of tenant gossip. She was offended by the insolent manner in which the garage attendants ignored her questions concerning the maintenance of her car, took their sweet time when it came to parking it and acted as though they couldn't care less whether or not it was actually stolen.

One session stands out in my mind with Merle arriving uncharacteristically late and disheveled-looking, her face slightly swollen and blotchy, the skin above her upper lip reddish with some very recent abrasions. Fighting back tears, she related how hours earlier she had been taking her customary morning walk along Queens Boulevard, daydreaming as usual, when her feet had suddenly shot out from under her, propelling her forward. She had landed directly on her face in the street. She could still remember the creepy sensation of the impact on the base of her nose and her initial panicky feeling that perhaps she had disfigured herself. Narrating this, she turned her face in profile so that I could better inspect her nose. "I don't think it's broken," she said hopefully. I conscientiously studied her nose which looked as straight as ever to me, but I was painfully aware I was a psychotherapist and not a physician. When

I suggested she visit a doctor after our session just to make sure, she shook her had impatiently. She had too many things she wanted to do on her day off and besides she had something else to tell me.

What she wanted to talk about to my surprise was not having fallen rather brutally on her face, but what happened next. When she had been helped to her feet by a passerby, escorted to the curb and delivered into the care of a woman who had been standing on the street corner about fifty feet away. This woman, who had watched the accident unfold, was the owner of a nearby flower shop and, apparently concerned, had invited Merle to come inside, rest and compose herself.

And it was this woman, whose initial offer of assistance and hospitality almost immediately evaporated when it became clear that Merle wanted to stay for more than a minute, whom she wanted to talk about. Unable to accept that anyone could be less than genuinely kind to her when she had just sustained a possibly broken nose and concussion, Merle recounted in painful detail how the shopkeeper—who obviously was trying to get rid of her—had repeatedly advised her to take a cab home and go to sleep; how she had glumly countered that she was too weak to get up from the chair which had been provided for her, but how, finally, unable to bear the woman's display of being put upon, in spite of feeling nauseous and faint, she had forced herself to leave the premises.

Merle's deep distrust and extreme sensitivity to the indifference of others—especially those who act out their real feelings under the cover of assuming a conventional authoritarian or paternal role—alerted me to the possibility for interpersonal control for someone who, as she put it, goes by the book. Accordingly, I paid increasing attention to the myriad instances in which people relate by rote. Here, allowing for many exceptions, is a simple profile of this kind of interaction:

1. Although obvious, it is important to note that the person who is going by the book in effect is denying that they are under the influence of any emotion or motivation other than a wish to properly discharge the responsibilities and carry out the duties of the job or task at hand. Given this initial, seemingly

innocent, but actually radical premise, it becomes possible to arbitrarily split their interpersonal world into "Just doing my job" and the equally important, "That's not my job." And, thereby, such a person acquires a limited but failsafe shield for being dismissive and disrespectful—so long as one is not excessively or officially rude—and getting away with it. That is, under the guise of informing or correcting the uneducated public, the putative role expert may really be trying to covertly humiliate the other by drawing attention to their ineptness.

From the standpoint of object relations, to go by the book is to enact a scripted role, devoid of spontaneity, in which interrelating is replaced by a series of well-practiced steps. The underlying assumption now is that what people do to and with one another is to be supposedly functional and instrumental: action and reaction intermeshing to produce a mutual benefit. In such a scenario, how one feels—relates to each interactional sequence in the performance of a specified role action (e.g., buying a commuter's ticket at a railway station)—is deemed irrelevant, if not downright intrusive.

As opposed to this, my point, and a theme of this book is that there is always a minimal intimacy and relational need that cannot be completely suppressed and that will to a certain extent shadow the functional performance. And since the customary exercise of the role, especially rote performance, dependent as it is on mindless repetition, often tends to be boring, the urge to express relational needs, fueled by frustration, may even become stronger. Yet, there may be no more effective way of denying this than by going by the book. By calling attention to the improprieties or infractions of a custom, rule or proper exercise of a social, business or professional role, an aura of expertise is imparted that deflects attention away from the underlying personal dynamics. More often than not the other becomes almost immediately defensive and lacks the confidence to challenge the person's true motives. And the fact that the other is ignorant, or at least feels so, makes it easy to exaggerate the trouble that is being caused by the other's alleged mistakes. For all these reasons, going by the book can be an appealingly simple way to psyche someone out.

2. It is also, as a corollary to the above, a justification for adopting a moralizing, pedagogic posture. Inasmuch as the essence of a rule or regulation is institutionalized repetition, as though testimony to its general acceptance, not knowing a rule can be unconsciously equated to not knowing the law (and, by the same logic which cautions ignorance of the law is no excuse, it may seem permissible to act morally superior to the supposed violator).

3. On another level, going by the book can represent an encapsulated interaction, a relational one-night stand with a known termination. Two people bonded by a common activity with a common instrumental goal, comforted in the knowledge that it will soon be over. From this standpoint role-relating is not unlike serial-relating, with its promise of a safe promiscuity (an unconscious denial of the underlying numbing repetitiveness).

4. And from the perspective of the theme of this book, it is easy to see that this kind of relating can create the illusion that one party is in charge, with knowledge at his fingertips, who has a precise answer to what the other needs to know. There is power in such an answer. Although on one level, both parties know perfectly well that it is only useful information that is being sought, on another level, reinforced by the unconscious attempt to suspend interrelating—a void that the desire for power can quickly fill—there is the sense that only mastery and understanding of the situation or task at hand is what matters and to the one who has it, therein lies a convincing, if fleeting, triumph.

5. It follows that someone who can go by the book, can also punish by the book. This becomes relatively easy to do because—under the cover that no real relationship exists in the first place—the person can behave as though they are simply following the rules, howsoever personal or punitive. In this scenario, the book, or rule that is not to be violated, assumes the authority of an external, auxiliary superego (somewhat suggestive of the wartime superego that Freud posited as taking over during periods of military strife). Should the other protest they feel deprived by the rigidity or arbitrariness of the behavior in question, the person can always claim, after all, that they are only reacting, not initiating. The

decision that laid the groundwork for what is now being enacted, was most likely made a long time ago.

In this respect, the enforcer of a rule or custom is like an officer of the court. Such a person can thereby disclaim agency for any discomfort experienced by the other, asserting their own supposed powerlessness to modify the rule. (The rule, so to say, does not allow it! It is the rule, therefore, which is not sufficiently flexible and sensitive to the needs of the other, not the enforcer of the rule. And, although the exercise of judgment in applying the rule cannot logically be counted out, the person can with equal logic claim that the area of the judgment call is itself circumscribed by the rule, which in this particular case happens not to be relevant. Furthermore, the enforcer can rationalize that he is not only not enforcing, he is applying a rule which in his view is so self-evidently clear-cut that the ambivalence necessitating a delicate exercise of judgment is entirely absent).

Such a defense might be called "Go fight City Hall" or "You want me to lose my job?" Any protest of personalized abuse is deflected to the code of rules, which is charged with being the true author of the alleged offense. If there is unfairness, it is in the rule and not in the hands of the one who has been empowered to enact it. Therefore it is the originator or custodian (e.g., City Hall) of the noxious rule who should be accosted and not its dutiful servant. Here the enforcer tries to form a counterfeit and self-serving alliance with the victim by claiming to be—albeit from a different angle—as controlled, compliant and harassed as the complainant. There is even the hint that the enforcer, inasmuch as his or her livelihood depends upon it, is more under the thumb of the prevailing regulations than the transient passerby. (This may explain, in part, the oft-noted arrogance of workmen in the street vis-a-vis pedestrians: i.e., this is my workplace and these are my tools. Analogously, the person who assumes a position of petty authority, seems to be saying—"I live with, by and under these rules. They are my territory, my work and you are just narcissistically reacting to a passing inconvenience.")

For all of these reasons, going by the book can seem to be little more than grandiose mindlessness. The other may be struck, whether consciously (as Merle was) or unconsciously, by the blatant stupidity of a transaction that is based on the power that inheres in the carrying out of a role: whether it is the power of a doorman to facilitate the traffic of occupants or visitors to a building, or a super who is to insure that the overall maintenance of the premises is upheld and attended to, or a shopowner who is to be the sole judge of who is welcome as a visitor and who is not. It seems stupid because it apparently represents an unquestioning identification with a manifestly insensate, impersonal rule (taken as an unconscious admission on the person's part that they are doing no original thinking at all but are simply complying with an inner mandate to behave in a specified manner).

However, since every dynamic, interpersonal situation feels different, the insistent repetitiveness of a typical power transaction cannot help but be perceived by the outsider as a galling oversimplification of a complex, current interaction. And it is part of the grandiosity of a power operation not to be aware—at least from the standpoint of relating—of its mindless, unidimensional character. It may be the use of power, analogous to the release of anger—which tends to depend on the first strike immobilization of the other's resources—rests on the unconscious belief that it can safely dispense with the need for cognitive strategizing.

Another defense against such glaring lack of sophistication is the prospect of savoring an immediate surge of power. After all, if you've just clearly put someone in their place, shown them who's boss, what difference does it make if they're critical of your way of doing it? Realistically, you expect them to be about as disgruntled as you would be in their shoes. There is therefore boastfulness behind the apparent stupidity of even the petty power broker: as though to say, "I have no need to be cunning with you—you do not require cunning." This, as I hope to show, is an essential ingredient of many power games. By seeming comparatively unafraid to resort to a candid display of power, the message is that authority, precedent and, if necessary, force—not argument, sentiment or emotion—will carry the day. It is comparable to the open-fist attitude of frank anger. For power does not feel like power if it has to be overly litigious or cerebral. By contrast, its actions proclaim—"This is the way it is, because this is the way it is (and no need to explain further)."

Not surprisingly, the relationship of thought, especially reflective thought, to power is ambivalent: while it may have been necessary in the past in order to establish the rationale and consolidate the original basis for the desired authority, it is considered superfluous in the present once power has been obtained (when the time is for action, not doubt, and when there is no need to think together). From this perspective, lack of certainty is a sign of vacillation, a transparent rationalization for avoiding a possible conflict of interests and part of the arrogance of someone who goes by the book is that they assume they know exactly what action is required, how to do it and how to consummate it. In other words they are intent upon controlling the pace of the transaction.

An exasperating aftermath of this upon the other is the helpless sense that they are to have no input into a situation which directly affects them. Although on the one hand the person who is arbitrarily exercising authority is supposedly the more knowledgeable—who can plausibly fall back on the justification that this is my job, my territory—the one who is suffering the brunt of the consequences of the action, and who will have to live with it, is the customer. While this is typically denied by the one in charge, who is likely to counter, "My job is at stake here"—it seems rare indeed when this is actually the case. Instead, there is usually considerably more leeway to be flexible than is admitted (the denial of which is therefore an effective ploy for discouraging and nipping in the bud the other's potential resistance). Finally, because the exercise of power by its nature tends to become routine—in spite of claims that they believe and are invested in doing what they do well—it is often, when all is said and done, a meaningless experience. Which can add salt to the wound: the one who is being dismissed may see that the person in charge, under the guise of just doing his job, but who could just as easily have chosen to do otherwise, is really enjoying the frustration he is causing.

Counter Strategy

When Merle left the flower shop, still uncertain as to whether her nose had just been broken, she felt humiliated for ever having allowed herself to believe that the owner was actually concerned for her welfare. Although she immediately reprimanded herself for not having asserted herself more, she also realized that it is extremely difficult to challenge someone who is making a show of sympathy, howsoever disingenuous. But what of the much more commonplace instance, wherein someone rightly or wrongly feels unfairly shunted aside, without apology, simply because the other has the power and is so inclined: to be passed over for a long sought-after promotion without a word of explanation; to have repeated telephone calls on an important personal matter not even returned; to have requests for basic, necessary information refused by a clerk who chooses to regard your questions as unacceptable intrusions upon his or her time; to be treated as though a lack of information or know how is a sign of stupidity or that an admission of a need for assistance is also an acknowledgment of dependency or confession of a readiness to be controlled?

Although few are willing to confront an individual who is perceived as a figure of even petty authority, such encounters of course do occur. At which time a frequent counter strategy by the one who feels trivialized and humiliated is: to try to puncture what is typically viewed as either officiousness, pompous posturing or moral sadism by emphasizing the here and now pain, discomfort and downright misery being incurred as a result of a seemingly mindless, by-the-book enforcement of a rule, regulation or a principle of behavior. By thereby dramatizing one's suffering one hopes to shake the power player out of his or her moralistic complacency and instead to make some kind of rudimentary, human contact. Someone who feels victimized struggles to get the other to relate to, identify and empathize with her and not, as is usually the case, to his sense of duty and obligation to an abstract regulation or impersonal process. In turn, the other may counter the counter strategy by manifestly affirming his identification with the function he is performing. So, on the one hand, there is a frustrated person who stresses she is to be regarded as a valid exception and, on the other hand, there is someone who asserts the need for regulations applying to all people who, typically, will flatly deny that the case in point calls for a legitimate exemption from the standard protocol (hinting instead that the person is avoiding responsibility for her evident ignorance or incompetence by overreacting and selfishly complaining).

From the standpoint of intimacy and relational distance, it is worth noting that two people could not be further apart: the one who is holding the reins of power can seem inhumanly indifferent to the suffering of the other, who in turn can just as easily seem contemptibly out of synch, misinformed and willfully disruptive. The profound emptiness that usually follows in the wake of the termination of this kind of a transaction, howsoever brief, can therefore be seen as a reflection of each party's perception of the other's radical lack of attunement and respect for their self. Often the party with power will defend against such emptiness by trying to savor the fleeting triumph over the other, while ignoring the obvious fact that his recent performance is being viewed as but another shameful instance of the abuse of power. By contrast, there is no similar compensation for the person who feels dismissed, who has a far more difficult time escaping the consequences of what is often perceived as a blatantly toxic interpersonal encounter (one recourse being to seek meaning by regarding oneself as an honorable victim).

THE VOICE OF EXPERIENCE

If Merle was oversensitive when it came to being treated in a peremptory fashion, she was positively phobic over the possibility of treading on the tender feelings of her ninth grade students by misusing her authority as a teacher. Despite ten years experience as an English teacher in one of the more prestigious private schools in Manhattan, she continued to search conscientiously for a teaching stance with which she could be comfortable. She especially agonized over finding the right admixture of discipline and nurturance, believing that one without the other was ineffective. Empathy, unless it was presented in a structural environment, was easy to disrespect and discipline, minus sensitivity, engendered resentment. Not surprisingly, Merle's forte—when it came to her personal equation for teaching excellence—was empathy and her solution (which never seemed to work) for incorporating the necessary dosage of discipline was to remind refractory students that what she said was backed by the weight of her experience.

"But no one listens to the voice of experience, at least when it's mine," Merle would sigh; typically, after failing dismally to stand up to the literal cross-examination of some unruly, smart-aleck student. Merle's impossible dream—to be kind and sensitive, empathic and nurturing without having to also occasionally frustrate her charges—represented for me a kind of basic conundrum confronting people who are eager to impart a particular store of hard-won, privileged knowledge.

For it is an understandable wish to provide someone you like, to whom you would want to give something of value, only the benefits, and not the pain of your experience. The wish is to somehow teach them about the pain, without them having to undergo it. And the hope is that they will trust you enough, that your account of your own suffering from your own mistakes will be sufficiently compelling so that they will be unable to slough it off.

After all, to believe that you already have under your belt years of essentially the same experience that developmentally lies in store in the case of the young—or that, due to special training or opportunity, you are experientially far advanced in comparison with certain less advantaged, uninitiated peers—is also to believe that you are a bit of a prophet, someone who is in a position to see the future of the other. Or rather to see that the future, to the extent it is believed to be unknown, is illusory because in reality it is only going to be a repetition, with expected variations, of your own past.

It is natural that the other will instinctively resist just such experiential future-telling, viewing it as both an appropriation and trivialization of whatever freshness and significance their own encounter with the future may hold. They may therefore be suspicious of possible ulterior motives: why, for example, do they doubt they will be up to mastering whatever contingencies the future presents without needing a guide to dilute or perhaps even delete the shock of raw experience? Do they feel that the other's life, or life in general, is best conducted if it is strategically envisioned rather than exploratively, adventurously, spontaneously and sometimes playfully encountered? Are they anti-surprise? Is their version of the good life one that can be calculated in advance?

In reaction to this, the person who is endeavoring to provide someone she cares about with only the benefits and not the pain of her experience will sense not only the other's resistance, but the intrinsic futility of her hope. For how do you teach from your own experience, if you wish to bar access to it? Learning from experience means learning from your experience or, to put it another way, to profit from personal past mistakes. What gives the results of experience their customary weight is analogous to what gives the carrying out of a key experiment its significance: that sense of encountering in a meaningful way the unknown and realizing the extent, for better or worse, that you have been changed (or enlightened).

Now this may be the central dilemma facing parents who are responsible for finding a way to educate their children, while saving them from the perils lying in wait but which they do not yet understand (e.g., the menace of a hot stove to an infant, the danger to a young child of being hit by an automobile in the street, and so on). To put it another way, how do they inculcate the benefits of experience without requiring them to learn from the pain of experience when the pain can be overwhelmingly destructive (being physically or psychically traumatized)? More often than not, the traditional parental solution is a bypassing rather than a resolution of this dilemma: that is, to rely on prohibition, rule, authority, intimidation and frank bullying ("do it, because I say so"). Although the child typically obeys, he or she does not understand the basis of their compliance. And to the noncompliant or stubborn child who wants and asks for more than instruction, the parent is likely to point to and then retreat behind the logic of authority, in effect claiming that, "I must be right because I have so much more life experience behind me."

Aside from saving their children from useless pain—accidental injuries, diseases, traumas—where the costs far outweigh the benefits of learning from experience, parents are faced with the even more daunting task of facilitating their development: i.e., providing the proper dosage of necessary new experience, which entails allowing them to take risks and thereby make meaningful mistakes from which hopefully they can learn, but which do not traumatically overtax them. It is obviously a fine line which parents need to negotiate—on the one hand to avoid being overprotective—and on the other to responsibly and sensitively monitor the amount of novel developmental experience which is to be made available to the uninitiated child.

Needless to say, few parents possess the patience or empathy required for this demanding task and instead fall back on what we have been terming the voice of experience. Such instances of our parents trying to intimidate us with the authority of their personal histories are not only remembered but internalized. As adults, it is a short step—when we have been challenged to explain our rationale for exercising some localized power which we have managed to acquire—to unconsciously emulate the bullying tactics resorted to in moments of sufficient stress by our parents.

"I USED TO BE THAT WAY"

This is a popular everyday power game that is a subtle variation of the Voice of Experience. Instead of pretending to be offering only the benefits and not the pain of experience, the person will stress their identification in the past with what the other is presently undergoing, but as a covert way of deflecting attention away from their aim which is to manipulate the other into changing their behavior when they do not really intend to. Thus someone complains that they are mired down in a job that they despise, in a relationship that does not seem to be going anywhere, in a lifestyle that gives them little or no pleasure. To which, the listener, apparently oozing with empathy, sighs, "I used to be that way."

Owning up, however, in such a matter-of-fact, undefensive manner to a seemingly hard truth, can often be no more than an instance of what I have termed narcissistic honesty: i.e., the grandiose belief that if one brazenly and publicly admits one's most glaring shortcomings (e.g., "I know I have a terrible temper") one is somehow thereby exonerated from the responsibility of remedying them. Typically, the other is initially disarmed by the candid admission suggesting a kinship of frailty and perhaps implying that a bond of some kind has already been formed. A very simple act of seductiveness that is used to screen what is really happening: that the person is thereby assuming a higher-level position, a greater authority for the purpose of talking down to the other. What the person is therefore actually saying is: I learned my lesson. I faced up to my problems, took responsibility for my situation, my feelings and did what I had to do to surmount it (and--here's the punch line--you should, too).

What's more, the apparent generosity of the person in sharing genuine flaws in his past is used to patch over the off-putting inference that now he is quite a different person from the other, and very happy to be different. In short, an appeal to their common experience is made in order to defuse the other's defensivenss—e.g., "I know what you're talking about"—while the claim of having the additional experience of recovering from past deficits (an experience which the other who is in the thick of her conflict obviously sorely lacks) is employed to legitimate the person's posture of authority.

For all of these reasons the other tends to feel deflated, often without knowing why. There can be a vague sense of having been put down together with an awareness that one is unsure as just how to confront one's aggressor. In extreme cases—when there is collusion with the person who is being disingenuous at best—the other may actually take heart and eagerly identify with someone who is now viewed as a possible mentor. (It is worth noting that parents, of course, are notorious, upon encountering resistance to their instructions—"Why do I have to do that?"—for reminding their children that they, too, once had to endure the deprivations of childhood.)

RADIO RELATING

Going by the book and the voice of experience are two common examples of how everyday relating can be converted into a rather obvious power game. At the other end of the continuum, are those instances (that I am terming radio relating) in which ordinary conversation—under the guise of being just an amiable wish to entertainingly wile away the time—can be manipulated to serve ulterior motives.

Since this is most clearly seen when relating is frankly regarded as an outright performance, there is probably no better example than that afforded by our current mania for titillating talk shows. As a veteran of mostly nonprofit, public service radio programs, in which I would be featured as a guest author, I can provide the following illustrative, personal anecdote.

I was to be appearing for the first time on Canadian radio to discuss the publication of my new book, having been invited by the assistant of the hostess, a well-known newscaster. The interview would be conducted on the telephone, which means I would be speaking from the privacy and comfort of my Manhattan office directly to the sound studio in Canada where it would be broadcast live. I was to be allotted between twenty to thirty minutes of air time and, as is often the case, I would not be meeting my hostess until minutes before the program began.

My main concern when the time arrived was whether my prospective interviewer had taken the trouble to review the promotional materials that had been forwarded to her by my publisher. I knew from experience that it was rare for a busy newscaster to actually read even a few pages from a book they were planning to publicly discuss, and that they preferred to rely upon pithy summaries, jacket copy and deceptively authoritative on air personas combined with a professional speaker's knack of winging it on almost any subject irrespective of the state of their ignorance.

In spite of that, and in keeping with my training as a therapist, I hoped to make a personal connection with my interviewer, if I could. I was therefore quick to ask her—when she had introduced herself to me just moments before the program was scheduled to begin—if she had had time to acquaint herself with the subject matter of my book. While unembarrassed to tell me she had only been able to leaf through it, she seemed eager to reveal that she herself had once been employed in the mental health field: "I once worked for eight months as a psychiatric nurse."

To my immediate regret, I took the bait, "How did you like it?"

"I walked out. They were all nuts."

"Uh-huh."

"Are you nuts, too?"

"I try not to be."

And my heart sank, as I realized with whom I was about to be publicly coupled: someone who had no interest in either me or my book, who most likely saw both as simply raw material for a show. My problem, however, was that I was constrained to try to socialize and relate to this woman before a listening audience of tens of thousands for a specified period of time.

When, right after the first break for station identification, a sound engineer hurriedly told me that—because I was "speaking too fast" and "couldn't be understood" (it was true my speech tended to accelerate when I was particularly ill at ease) my air time was going to be cut short to only eight minutes—I was inwardly relieved.

Later, when I was able to review a tape of the broadcast which had been sent to me as a courtesy for my participation, I perceived perhaps for the first time what I had only dimly been aware of in my previous appearances as a guest author. To wit, that talk is considered primarily as an event, to be orchestrated and manipulated into a commodity as entertaining and immediately gratifying to listeners as possible. From such a perspective, the relationship per se is only an object to be exploited. Analogous to the artist's relationship to his material—in which everything is evaluated according to its usability for future aesthetic shaping and nothing is related to for itself—media relating is continuously being monitored, and revised, for its utility and projected appeal for media consumption.

To put it another way, the relationship exists not for itself but for the benefit of the audience, which means that it is a performance. As such it is completely subservient to time—has to occur within the constraint of predetermined sound bites—which means there can be no autonomous input regarding when it begins and when it ends. Although spontaneity of expression is valued, it is something that must take place within a rigid time frame. This, of course, is the antithesis of the spontaneity that is the hallmark of everyday intimate exchanges where time tends to be a servant of the interpersonal process.

From this standpoint, the cramming of everything into marketable sound bites represents the ultimate conversational reductionism—the arrogant attempt to apply what are believed to be the guidelines for entertaining expressiveness to the natural, open-ended unconscious flow of communication. And this cannot be done unless the following assumptions have been made (by the newscaster, station manager and whoever else determines policy): that it is already understood what an audience wants to hear, what comprises the dynamics of an entertaining dialogue and what are the techniques for repairing or enhancing a lackluster performance.

Although few would dispute that there is such a thing as legitimate expertise in appraising and sometimes improving a given media performance, what is often overlooked is the cost of acquiring such expertise: the giving up or denial of the unconscious world of exploratory communication, the hope that something both real and unknown could transpire, and the possibility that there could be growth. What is therefore ironic and ultimately toxic in media relating—when carried to the extreme as seen by today's so-called shock jocks— is the sometimes utter disregard for the impact upon the sensibilities of the participants. The upshot is that what is normally the most private and intimate attribute of a person has now been appropriated by an external agency to serve indifferent or intrusive ends tantamount to the true self being commanded to perform for the sole benefit of an exploitative other.

This is the dilemma that the individual artist (as I discuss in *Portrait of the Artist as a Young Patient*, Alper, 1997) partly escapes through dividing his labors into the solitary making of a uniquely personal product and the subsequent coming to terms with the demands of the market. The dilemma, of course, cannot be so neatly escaped by the performing artist, someone who—every dynamic second—must court the needs of the audience in order to elicit the sought after esthetic response. And to pursue the analogy, radio relating is like the performing artist at his or her commercial, worst level where there is almost no pretense that what is being performed is a work of art, but instead is regarded as conversational raw meat to be incessantly fed to a bored, stimulus-hungry audience craving pseudo-relationship snacks.

Although comparatively few people are afforded the opportunity of appearing on radio, the experience of regarding one's conversation—when there is a strong opportunistic motive for so doing—as a performance of a certain kind is, in my view, an almost universal occurrence. And, from the standpoint of our theme, when conversation passes from being an expression of what Christopher Bollas has termed the simple self (1993) to something that is to be used functionally, and especially narcissistically, it unconsciously is transformed into a power game.

"I HAVE A LOT OF PROBLEMS"

Ten years later, in therapy, Brook could chronicle the event, provide a step-by-step narrative of the day that she regarded as the worst of her life. It began with her mother's urgent telephone call from her home in Connecticut. Something was wrong, terribly wrong with Brook's younger sister, Phoebe, who was behaving in a "weird and frankly disgusting manner": walking naked from room to room while singing and sometimes speaking to herself, emptying out dresser drawers of clothes on the floor, rearranging items of furniture in the house in a nonsensical fashion, and finally attempting to telephone the police to inform them that a serial killer had recently moved into the neighborhood.

By the time Brook had arrived, seven frantic hours later, at the doorstep of her mother's house, a great deal had happened. The police had indeed come, but to take Phoebe away to the psychiatric ward of a nearby hospital, where she was met by a psychiatrist who had been contacted by the family physician and who wasted little time in diagnosing her as a manic depressive and arranging for her commitment.

Twelve days later when Phoebe was released in the care of her mother, Brook could see for herself that her sister had changed. Although the lithium that had been prescribed for her had done what it was supposed to do—stabilize her mood and reduce the expression of psychotic symptoms—never had Phoebe seemed so zombie-like. It was a lifelessness that abated only slightly when she was taken off the lithium several months later. It was a lifelessness that far surpassed in intensity the states of moody lethargy that Phoebe would drift into so often as a teenager.

Three months after her episode the twenty-year-old Phoebe startled her family by announcing she would not be returning to the University of Connecticut to begin her sophomore year. She would be recuperating instead in the privacy of her second-storey bedroom, the one she used to share with her sister but which now, ever since Brook had moved to Manhattan in order to become a cabaret singer, was hers alone. It was a recuperation that, ten years later, would be deemed still unfinished by Phoebe.

Faithfully, at least once a month, Brook would return home to spend the weekend. She resented the obligation she felt to cheer up her sister and her mother, to break through the chronic gloom that seemed to engulf them. She could not, and would not understand why Phoebe had restricted herself to her bedroom: incessantly listening to music or reading, occasionally venturing from the house to work a random shift as a waitress in a nearby restaurant or drop in (when she felt the need to socialize) on a local recovery group for the mentally ill.

In therapy, Brook repeatedly and bitterly complained about being held hostage to her sister's willful, if unconscious malingering. There could be nothing therapeutic, she would insist, in clinging to a vegetative, cocoon-like existence, abetted by a traumatized mother who was terrified that the slightest pressure might catapult her daughter back into a second major manic depressive attack. To undermine what she regarded as a destructively collusive mind-set, Brook would voice her nagging suspicions in private conversations with her mother that Phoebe may not have suffered an actual, full-blown psychotic episode. Or that, even if she had, there was absolutely no reason—especially in light of the fact that ten episode-free years had now safely gone by—to continually behave as though she were in danger of an imminent relapse. Might it not be better, Brook would argue, to gently but firmly encourage Phoebe to stop treating herself as a psychic invalid, to instead gradually reintroduce herself to the real world in which people worked as well as played, where there was both risk and opportunity, obligation and choice, pain as well as pleasure?

And this is what Brook, to no avail, tried to instill in her sister in the walks they would take, in the conversations they would have, during the outings they would sometimes go on. There was no need for therapy, Phoebe would argue, therapy was for people who wanted to do something in the world, who had goals, and she had none. She was happy not to be sick, to listen to music, to be alive, and besides, if she needed support, she always had the recovery group. And when Brook—invariably exasperated at what she viewed as a perversely negative outlook—challenged her sister as to how she could possibly be satisfied with a maintenance-level existence, Phoebe would fall back on her trump card, her failsafe exemption from having to face the rigors of life: "Well, I have a lot of problems."

Although, of course, I realized this was an extreme case, I thought it well illustrated the kind of dynamics that can be enacted when a relationship is approached from the standpoint of crisis intervention (whether real or imagined). When that is the case, the one who considers herself in special, dire need and therefore requiring special treatment, typically does not solicit help on the basis of whether the other wants to—as, for instance, in an attempt to facilitate mutuality—but on the basis that an SOS has just been sent. In such a context, saying no is scarcely an expression of autonomy, but an act of betrayal.

One therefore appeals not to the other's need for intersubjective enrichment, but to their sense of compassion for the downtrodden. By acknowledging that one is in distress, perhaps close to the end of their tether, it is implied that--since it is shameful to admit and natural to cover this up—it must be true. To accuse such a person of being less than honest—of being melodramatic, overreactive, or aggressively manipulative (which is often the case)—is to thereby seem mean-spirited. Furthermore, there is the implication that because she has lowered her guard and been so excessively open, she is entitled to trust.

Thus, whatever unfinished business, narcissistic injuries, and relational hardships have been suffered in the past are to be put in brackets: an appeal for help has been made—not on the basis of the history of the relationship, what has been consolidated between them and has, so to speak, been earned—but to the conscience. There is to be reparation for whatever the other could have done, but didn't, to avert the person's present downfall. The assumption is that the other is morally implicated and has no choice but to get involved. The other is somehow responsible, analogous to how he or she may feel unconsciously to blame for the plight of any heart-rending beggar one encounters. That is, one is at fault either for—although one may have been charitable in the past—obviously not having been charitable enough to have prevented the misfortune staring one in the face, or having been indifferent enough to have allowed the current catastrophe to occur.

For all of these reasons, there is the implicit demand that now the pain and the need can no longer be ignored and there cannot be any excuse for being uninvolved. Unconsciously inviting someone to rescue you, therefore, is like inviting someone to your psychic sick bed, wherein lies unmistakable proof of your pain and need. To do that, however, is to covertly realign the relational perspective: from being appraised as an intermediate space for two subjectivities to spontaneously make contact to one that is assessed according to its capacity to alleviate distressing symptoms. One might plausibly call this the medical model of relating--relational deficiencies as such are to be considered only diagnostic signs of an underlying psychological illness (rather than an inhibition against or an inability to relate and be intimate). And the message is that what needs to be done first is to address the core disease. Generally overlooked are the hidden assumptions and the dynamic interaction that can occur between someone and the real or imagined locus of their illness, to which I now turn:

A PERSON AND THEIR PSYCHIC PAIN SEEN AS
AN INTERNAL OBJECT RELATION

1. The immediate goal—getting the pain to stop and stopping it from doing any further damage—is typically the *only* goal. Any other project, such as working on a damaged relationship, must follow on the heels of this crucial first step.

2. The person is almost always at a disadvantage vis-a-vis his or her pain: it seems either impersonal and inscrutable (no matter how familiar, there is always a surprise factor to real pain, otherwise it would not be as upsetting as it is) or it appears meaningless (pain generally does not fit into a sensible context but seems to have arisen randomly). It may be, therefore, that the frequent attempt to explain pain to the self--as a consequence of ill-advised behavior on one's part, as retribution (e.g., bad karma returning), as being psychosomatic in origin or just psychically caused (imagined)--is an unconscious effort to appropriate agency, and thereby lend meaning, to something that apparently has come from the blue.

3. Pain is often unconsciously experienced as emanating from an amoral part of the psyche or an indifferent external universe. Because it can be in extreme cases so merciless and relentless it can feel cruel or evil. Its mindless, repetitive nature, without much variation or complexity, makes it seem as though whatever caused it was not conscious of or concerned with its end state impact: i.e., it's origin is inhuman. As opposed to ordinary emotions such as anger, joy, fear and grief it is linked in the psyche with traumatic anxiety and depression that under certain conditions can be abnormally stressful.

THE INFLUENCE OF PSYCHIC PAIN ON THE OTHER

The most common reaction is to almost immediately give up on any prospects one had for receiving nurturance from the relationship. Instead, there is often an attempt to do damage control combined with some guilty rumination. How much, if anything, is owed to this person? To what extent should someone pay heed to a request for rescue that unconsciously may be received as a latent threat of blackmail ("if you turn your back on me now, you will have to answer to your conscience")? Approached this way, it is easy to feel you are being asked to answer an eleventh hour prayer: i.e., "I've tried everyone else. You're my last hope."

There are some common counter moves employed by the other when it seems obvious that the pain that a person is in is being used as a power game. The other may then alternately downplay the urgency of the situation ("it's not a crisis") or their own actual ability to perform the desired rescue operation ("I really can't help you even if I wanted to...." "I'm having a bad time. I don't have any money.") The other may resort to gamesmanship, accusing the person of being histrionic, of malingering, of trying to avoid responsibility. The other may minimize the closeness of the past relationship because he or she does not want to be exposed for an inability to come through or remain loyal in a genuine crisis.

Relating then becomes a curious dynamic of witness, prosecution and defense wherein the underlying motivation is to defuse accusation and avoid anxiety-producing guilt. The person who wants to be saved will think in terms of relief from her real or imagined crisis and not in terms of interacting. Relational needs as such are then pushed into the background and the other is thought of as only an accessory to the inner turbulence or as a tool to contain it.

"LET US PRAY"

Although traditionally, and in theory, the process of psychotherapy—except for pastoral counselors and various practitioners of New Age spiritualism—does not depend on a belief in God for its power to heal, it is by no means simple to separate the secular from the religious when it comes to the consulting room. I am reminded, in particular, of a deeply religious patient who came to see me in a state of crisis. Although frankly skeptical of the value of therapy, he felt he had reached the end of the line in his marriage of eleven years, and had nowhere else to turn.

Because he was of Middle Eastern origin and adhered to a fundamentalist belief that women should be subject to the domination of their husbands, he could not accept that it had been his wife who had insisted on the breakup, who had in fact thrown him out of his own house and who, in the most unbearable insult of all, had boldly invited her new lover to move in with her. In an agitated depression he described how he had waited in the shadows across the street from his house to make sure for himself whether the rumors he had heard were true; how, when he had seen with his own eyes in the lighted bedroom window the man who had once been his friend, he had lost all reason and control, taking the baseball bat he had brought along and repeatedly smashing it against the side of his wife's car. "I wanted to kill her, so I killed the car instead," he told me with a kind of weary pride at the conclusion of his tale of betrayal, as though this proved—contrary to his wife's allegations—that he was capable of restraint and therefore still civilized.

To my surprise, a few hours after this initial session, his wife telephoned me in my office. She wanted me to know that the marriage was indeed over, that she had contacted a lawyer who had initiated divorce proceedings and had already obtained a police restraining order against her husband. Yet, though she was truly terrified of her husband's violent temper she wanted to meet with both of us in my office in the hope that—with the mediation of therapy—a more peaceful closure to what had been for her an insane ordeal might be reached.

With various reservations, but encouraged by the fact my patient was manifestly calmed down by his estranged wife's proposal to at least be with him in the same room, I agreed to a single joint session. As it turned out, the session was far less stressful than I had anticipated and even somewhat productive. But it was the remarkable way that it commenced—something I had never before, or afterwards, experienced in all my years as a therapist—that I cannot help remembering.

Sitting together on the couch, they looked at one another sadly and thoughtfully. "Can we pray?" my patient asked in a pleading voice, with the utmost tenderness. Nodding softly, his wife accepted his hand and then solemnly glanced downwards as he did, as they both palpably seemed to disappear within themselves before my eyes. In a few moments, my patient broke the meditative silence by reciting his prayer in a loud, trembling voice, which was followed by his wife's quite different prayer, befitting her New Age orientation, delivered in a no less spiritual but far more dispassionate tone.

Perhaps what had most impressed me was how uncharacteristic, how against the grain of the process of psychotherapy, at least as I knew it, was this brief spiritual interlude. It was not that their prayers were not heartfelt. On the contrary, they were poignantly so. It was just that the sentiments they expressed and, especially, the relationship they expressed, did not bear any resemblance to the actual one being enacted before me. I was aware, of course, that religious intimacy, the enactment of belief in a transcendental being, is a relationship apart from all others, but it did not hit home how different until I was able to observe them side by side: the merely human and interpersonal against the so-called supernatural. (It should be noted that what follows is a *psychological* discussion of a person's belief in and relationship to an hypothesized deity and is not intended as a philosophical contribution to the question of the existence of God.)

As a beginning, it is worth noting Adam Phillips' remark (*Terrors and Experts*, 1996) that in order for values, such as religious ones, to remain fixed, it is necessary they be distant. In other words, it is difficult up close not to observe difference and change. By contrast, a relationship with a deity is a relationship with a being you never see or experience in any of the ways by which you interact with everyone else. It is a relationship in which—although every aspect of your self or soul is known in advance—you cannot know (and are considered presumptuous to even try to guess) a single thought or feeling of the Other. Not only is there almost nothing in common, there is an infinite developmental difference between the believer and his or her God. Is it possible, therefore, to empathize and with whom?

Although it is taken for granted that there are profound differences between religious and interpersonal intimacy, it is illuminating to actually elucidate them. The entire life of a religious person, for example, from a certain metaphysical perspective, can be viewed as a spiritual performance or test, upon which final judgment will be passed in the afterlife. Other than the gift of life, nothing more is required from God. While prayers can be offered, no demands can be made. Traditionally, a believer is to be faithful to only one God who, however, is free to have a similar relationship with billions of others. Within the context of the ongoing religious relationship, there is to be no direct expression and interchange of emotion, and no simple sensuous (tactile) comforting. It is more accurate to say the relationship is one of searching, rather than having. Fittingly, love for a being as elusive as God is expressed—not in spontaneous interacting—but through meditative acts of worship.

But what of the part that is assigned in the religious relationship to God? Although the issues about to be raised, for all I know may have already been thoroughly debated in esoteric tracts by theologians, they are by no means in the forefront of the consciousness of the typical believer. And this is because they have not been taught, are not deemed relevant to the practice of faith and, perhaps most important of all, are not easily understandable. Nevertheless, to some extent, in my view, they are considered in the unconscious of every believer.

With that as a preamble, now on to the questions that rarely are asked, at least publicly, in traditional religious circles. Is there, for example, any benefit or growth that accrues to God from his involvement with human beings? Does He ever express needs or only demands? Is it the case that God may want, but does not need the love of people? And what possible use can a Deity, who has everything, have for people? Can there be room in such an odd couple—person and Deity—for spontaneity, playfulness, engagement—or is the relationship, as such, in the afterlife to come, to be only one of witness and presence? Can the essence of a Divinity allow for a sense of humor?

The Jehovah of the Old Testament expresses anger, rage, jealousy, a desire for vengeance. He renders judgment, vents fierce disapproval and savagely punishes enemies. The God of the New Testament, by contrast, emphasizes love and forgiveness. What is interesting, however, are the emotions and states of mind that the Bible *does not show* God as having: indecision, doubt, vulnerability, anxiety, fear and happiness. To me, as a psychoanalytic psychotherapist, it is at least worth asking—does God have an unconscious? And if not, as I think is suggested in the Bible, can He experience shock, surprise, or relief?

By contrast, the God of religious dogma in his relationship to humankind is primarily revealed through displays of divine approval or disapproval. He is depicted as: self-contained, grateful to no one or nothing; masculine in gender, as father or incarnated son, but without a specific sexual identity, character or personality. He is not only never ill and never tempted—except for his brief sojourn as Christ on earth—but presumably is immune from disease. And other than his original struggle with Satan, He does not experience conflict. The question becomes what kind of relationship is possible with a Deity that is utterly beyond the pale of human experience? The question is compounded by the fact that there is no other God with whom to compare this historical God (outside of the gods of comparative religion, of course) and therefore no real room for discrimination and choice. And traditionally the question of faith is not presented as an option. The initiate is taught from the beginning that there is no such thing as honest skepticism. There is only belief, a state of grace, or the mortal sin of the atheist's despair. The initiate cannot disbelieve, *must* love and cannot abandon the practice of the religion that has been passed on without incurring a formidable punishment.

For all of these reasons—from a purely psychodynamic point of view—the relationship between a believer and his or her God is subject to rather remarkable restraints. Perhaps foremost is the extraordinary mystery that surrounds it, in which much of the time is necessarily spent trying to pin it down, to fathom and gather one's true thoughts and feelings towards God, while attempting to guess how God views the person or may at the time of reckoning. You could say, therefore, that as a relationship—which traditionally can only become fully realized in the afterlife—it never really beings, but is rather a preparation, an expectation or fantasy of what such a beginning might be (as clearly implied in the famous question—"what would you say were you to meet God?"). It follows that a good part of a religious person's fear of God comes from their uncertainty as to what ultimately lies behind the mystery of existence. Or to put it another way, the believer cannot help at times but be haunted by the question—just how friendly, understanding and empathic will the God that one eventually meets really be?

Because of the above, this relationship that is depicted in religious dogma--especially in light of the concept of original sin—can at times be seen as one of profound mutual distrust. If, on the one hand, from the perspective of God (as imagined, of course, by an infinitely fallible human being)—at any moment a given person, by exercising free will and choosing evil, is capable of falling into original sin—it is hard to see how much confidence He can have in humankind. If, on the other hand, from the point of view of mere mortals—where ordinary acts of evil are theoretically punishable by sentencing to some kind of hell—one wonders where there is room to relax, and how can there be such a thing as an acceptable mistake? In other words, can God be truly offended and yet not resort to punitive action? Or, considering that the stakes are so high, are mistakes and the concept of working on a relationship irrelevant and only sins, their confession and possible forgiveness the only thing that matters? If this is the case, it is difficult to see, from the standpoint of the believer, how one can trust a Deity who never gives feedback, about whom you are clueless as to what He really thinks and feels about you, and who applies an infinitely high standard of morality to your behavior that may or may not be tempered by equal measures of infinite love and mercy.

How, then, do you love a Being who wields such incredible power over you and whom you fear so much? Looked at this way, the relationship seems fundamentally based on morality, on issues of good and evil, rather than, as is the case between ordinary people, on the interest and pleasure that is generated by the encounter. It follows if what is up for grabs is whether one's soul is to be saved or not, then nothing else seems important. Yet, although it seems self-evident that the believer will perennially be troubled by questions of his or her faith in the existence and ultimate goodness of God, no one apparently is threatened by the quality of God's faith in people. That is to say, there is no expectation of God *trusting* that a particular person who, let us say, has just committed a mortal sin will sooner or later come to his or her senses. Instead, God, with divine patience, waits to see whether the exercise of free will results in good or evil acts (although paradoxically He knows this already) and then, supposedly, responds with corresponding approval (love and forgiveness) or disapproval (readiness to punish).

From a psychoanalytic point of view this is highly suggestive of the primitive defense mechanism called splitting—where the object is divided into all good and all bad aspects. It is worth noting that in the traditional picture of religious dogma God does not relate to a mixture of good and evil. Mirroring this, the believer is essentially in a state of grace or heading that way or in sin and therefore in mortal danger. Someone in a state of grace is to be the recipient of infinite love. Someone in a state of unconfessed sin, unlucky enough to die that way, faces the greatest possible alienation from the love of God. But someone formerly in sin, who sincerely repents, may become the recipient of infinite mercy and forgiveness.

Regarding God's trust, therefore, it could be said that there is no need for it. Being perfect, omnipotent, seeing the future in its entirety, He knows everything there is to know. Absolute certainty supersedes the need for trust and belief. A good question, therefore, is can God also dispense with faith? Does God have or require faith in himself? Or, once again, is the profound importance of faith promulgated in religious doctrine a completely non-reciprocal obligation, something imposed only on the believer? And, although the question is typically ignored, it can be asked—does God's omniscient ability to foretell the future equally apply to his own thoughts, actions, and emotions?

I think it is clear that what is missing from this conventional portrait of a divine persona, is the recognition of the profound and pervasive *ambivalence* that characterizes all human relations, especially transcendental ones. It is therefore hardly surprising that, traditionally, purity of heart is demanded from would-be believers, but that is exactly what no human really has. Is there empathy then for the ordinary person, neither good nor evil, who somewhat struggles but does not reach any clear stance vis-á-vis religious belief and commitment? The fact that man's relationship to God is primarily cast in the trappings of a cosmic morality play—with archetypal principles of good and evil battling for the soul of the person, with God waiting and watching, the all-seeing Judge, occasionally intervening with revelations, miracles, stupendous acts of grace, forgiveness— hides the basic psychological truth that so far as an object relation is concerned, there does not seem room in it for commonplace, undramatic failure, indecision, confusion, lack of development, stubborn refusal to change, demoralization, withdrawal. In short, there does not seem to be recognition of all the impediments to the achievement of genuine intimacy that universally plague people and, especially, there does not seem to be nearly enough room to work on all the daunting, extraordinary impediments to religious intimacy in a human, non-miraculous fashion.

It follows this startling absence of ambivalence and conflict in the traditional concept of a Divinity is taxing to the imagination of mere mortals. For while God, by definition, can do and be anything, the perception of Him is certainly limited by the constraints of human understanding. And these constraints are quickly reached as one comes face to face with unanswerable questions once one begins seriously to explore what it means to be a divine being. For example, God being omniscient, is there a need for Him to think? After all, thinking implies there is something worth thinking about, something one would like to know more about, and understand better, but if God is already omnipotent and omniscient, it is difficult to see what unsolved problems there are left to think about. In lieu of active cogitation, is there simply timeless contemplation of all the beauty and magnificence of everything He knows? Does God, therefore, have no past and was always exactly as He is, or was there development? Did He make Himself and, if so, how difficult was the task? What is the meaning of the infinite discrepancy between the perfectability of humankind and its Deity and why, for example, if it is true that God made man in his image, did He not do a much better job: make creatures that were much closer if not equal to Him in terms of omnipotence? Is there an implied master-slave relationship; are human beings as fallible as they are because that is their nature or is there a divine need for the extraordinary distance between believer and Deity?

For all of these reasons, the transcendental relationship, even in the best case scenarios, is characterized by profound uneasiness. From that standpoint, the obsessional rituals that so often inform religious practice, may be seen as attempts to fill an objective existential void: created by the unconscious fear of the religious person that God as a divine object will die—either because the abnormal distance separating the object of worship becomes too great to support, requiring too much of an investment of faith, or because the fantastic abstractness of the God concept finally succumbs to a kind of tautological meaninglessness. This may be why hostility towards or negative identification with God so often is expressed nihilistically and, especially, ontologically: God does not exist.

As an antidote to the crisis of faith to which a believer is always at least partially susceptible, the obsessional practice of religious rituals can serve to numb ontological doubts with their mindless and concrete repetitiveness. Their gross, but reassuring serial representation—behavioral reminders of an unseen spiritual relationship—can temporarily mute skepticism regarding the nagging question of the existence of God. It is worth noting that since there is, by definition, no perceptual basis or sensory immediacy to a transcendental relationship, it requires psychic work to maintain a plausible sense that what is supposed to be happening, is really happening. Rituals are meant to provide that plausibility by offering boundaries and clear-cut guidelines—telling us how to act, what to say and how to feel.

From such a perspective, prayers can be viewed as the special language that one needs to learn in order to speak to God; and spiritual receptivity is the ability one must have in order to understand the message God is wont to send. While priests are the teachers, translators and interpreters of God's language.

Is there room in the transcendental domain for dissent, for the one who cannot or will not believe? If perhaps the greatest possible repudiation of what was supposed to be a romantic, intimate commitment is the retrospective disclaimer, "I never loved you"—analogously—the gravest rebuke of an erstwhile religious devotee is the declaration, "I do not believe in the existence of God." This is far weightier than the former, human, all-too-human case, not only because the object of worship is supposedly of infinitely greater significance, but because the denial is totalistic, encompassing even prior existence: at least the rejecting person who proclaims, "I never loved you" does not deny that both participants truly existed. (This is one powerful reason why the disbeliever's fear of divine retribution can be so unsettling--if a mistake has been made, and one can never prove God does not exist, then one has unwittingly delivered the ultimate metaphysical insult to God.)

It follows that the urgency of proving one's loyalty through acts of worship combined with the fear of the terrible consequences for acts of betrayal, constitutes, from a psychodynamic standpoint, the lynchpin of the believer's relationship to his or her Deity. But if this is so, the question suggests itself—to what extent can someone love God, while simultaneously dreading Him? As a corollary to this there is the question—is it possible to love God without fearing him at all? And is it ever appropriate to be angry with or to express anger at God?

Is it possible to have a close relationship to Him and yet be independent of His approval? Carrying this further, to what extent can someone have a relationship with God and still be one's own person? Can someone, who has been deeply religious, suddenly initiate a divorce—perhaps a trial separation—from God without incurring divine retribution? Can one, other than praying for help, request (say for the purpose of clarification) some autobiographical information concerning God? Is it ever possible to have a non-reverent or a playfully irreverent, relaxed time with one's Deity? Or, can one acknowledge God's omnipotence and yet, howsoever irrationally, quarrel with particular instances of its manifestation? How, then, finally, does one challenge an infinite being? (And yet, of course, one does: by defiantly insisting on one's right to think small—that is, to be narcissistic.)

Although it is therefore almost impossible to imagine sanctioned outlets for the expression of anger towards Divinity within the traditional conception of the believer's position vis-á-vis God, it is easy to imagine heretical ones. A person so inclined may simply doubt, disbelieve and in general alienate himself from his former spiritual values. He may take advantage of the distance implicit in religious deference and intensify it to the point of aloofness and unreality. He may capitalize on the deferred status of the afterlife with its promise of a real relationship to God—to defer belief itself. After all, if one has to wait until the next life to meet God, one might as well wait until then to take religion seriously. One thereby unconsciously uses the non-reciprocal nature of the transcendental relationship to justify a skeptical wait-and-see attitude. Since God does not speak, make direct contact, intervene or punish directly, one therefore may also not speak and does not have to frankly embrace or deny the existence of a Deity. With some impunity, a person can procrastinate, dealing with the hereafter in a way one never can in a secular world in which there is typically immediate feedback and consequences for one's actions or failures to act.

If this is so, it may be that atheism is unconsciously rationalized as a person simply calling a spade a spade, and an absence an absence: that is, the conclusion is drawn that the reason one does not hear, see or touch God and often feels no such divine presence exists, is because no one is there. Thus the atheist, so he or she thinks, has the courage, which the believer lacks, to confront God's absence. From a psychodynamic standpoint, it could be said that the atheist is under the influence of the defense mechanism of projective identification: a lack of God's presence felt as a rejection of the person's worth too painful to contain is projected back into the universe, identified with and then experienced as a certainty that there is no God. It is as though the atheist unconsciously protests, "If I have to wait to meet God, He can wait, too—until He proves His existence by becoming present—to meet me." We can see the astuteness in Julia Kristeva's (Phillips, 1994) question—"Is atheism depressed?" (and a parallel question might be—is faith manic?).

I realize, as I have mentioned, that this strange catalogue of questions I have been raising—especially those speculating upon God's point of view regarding human beings—are almost never broached, if at all, outside of esoteric theological tracts. This, I believe, is not because they are considered heretical, but because they are manifestly unanswerable and do not seem to go anywhere. My point, however, is the fact they are inscrutable does not prevent them--howsoever dimly and unconsciously—from being considered. And the more deeply religious a person is the more difficult I believe it is to avoid the shadow of such questions. If we think about it from the perspective of the true believer—the fate of whose soul possibly throughout all of eternity is at stake, but where there is absolutely no divine feedback—who can traditionally only know the verdict when it is too late to do anything about it, on Judgment Day, it is impossible not to be susceptible, to a greater or lesser extent, to a desperate need to at least guess how one's God may feel or think about him or her.

Here, the dilemma facing the believer is that one can only endeavor to comprehend infinity on the basis of one's own finite experience, which means the only possible way to try, howsoever dimly, to understand how God views you, is to compare the relationship to every other one you have ever known. And in all of these, the crucial component has been feedback, especially feedback involving thought and feeling.

The believer who aspires to authentic religious intimacy is, therefore, faced with the incredibly daunting task of risking everything, investing everything in a Supreme Being whose essence by definition is unknowable and whose ultimate apprehension of you is forever shrouded in mystery. In saying this, I am aware, of course, of the concept of grace in which communion with God supposedly can exist in spite of the ordinarily formidable obstacles, but such exemption, it is generally agreed, is given only to a few.

As just one example of how the unanswerableness of certain existential or theological questions has never prevented anyone from asking them, consider this: the fact that no one has yet come back from the dead has failed to deter anyone, who is not mentally disabled, from wondering what it might be like to no longer be alive. From a psychoanalytic point of view—in which, as mentioned, death does not exist in the unconscious—there is, of course, ample reason for at times being morbidly preoccupied with questions regarding the afterlife. For if we cannot, psychically, conceive of somehow not being partially alive after we have died, then we are vulnerable to ruminations about what might be termed *the lonesomeness of being dead*: in which there are two great losses—the loss of everything in this world and the loss of the opportunity to be comforted for this greatest loss of all by being able to mourn. For whom could you tell and by whom could you be consoled? While none of us knows what may or may not lie in store for us after we die, there is a consensus that we will be incapable of discussing it in our customary earthly fashion with anyone we have ever known.

For some reason, major religions seem to have deleted this and taken as their primary task the instruction, indoctrination and induction of their devotees into the next world. They forget that, unconsciously, anyone who is in the process of dying, no matter how devout, first needs to mourn the total loss of this world—and, especially, when they have been presumably awakened in the afterlife—before they are ready to initiate a relationship with a radically altered realm of experience. And this, I suggest, may be one of the primary obstacles to religious belief; not that they cannot metaphysically accept the postulated afterlife, but that they know, unconsciously, they cannot possibly meet the traditional religious demand that they leave this world completely and then proceed instantly to take up a new life in another world without being granted a fraction of the seemingly infinite psychic time required to mourn the totalistic, cosmic bereavement they have just incurred.

In light of the above, it is hard to see how undue respect, if not fear, of divine power cannot be an integral part of the true believer's relationship to his or her Deity. If this is so, from the standpoint of our theme, to a greater or lesser extent, the dynamics of power—of which the enactment of power games is always a part—must sooner or later come into play.

ONE-UPMANSHIP

In an overcrowded and competitive society such as ours where so many people seem bent on finding a winning advantage, acknowledging vulnerability may be considered a strategic blunder. Indeed, it is a basic tenet of the philosophy of one-upmanship that one never admits to being in a one-down position. At the other end of the continuum, however, is the person who enters therapy, someone who—in the hope of gaining relief from psychic turbulence-- may be only too eager to narrate (and often overdramatize) the frailties of the self. Psychotherapy can therefore be a window to the other side, the dark side of one-upmanship, what Christopher Lash (1979) once aptly termed the 'culture of narcissism'. It can do this by showing the manifold toxic ramifications to the self of the person who has been variously demeaned, trivialized, coerced, manipulated and reduced by the other. The ways of demeaning the individual do not have to be devious, disguised or complex (in fact, it is a hallmark of a power game, as mentioned, that it shuns cunning, regarding it as a tactic of the weak). These ways can therefore be as simple, and widespread, as not bothering to return a telephone call, presuming that whatever the other wants to say somehow cannot be really serious (e.g., "What's up?"), denying that one wishes to be superficially gratified by adopting a tone of pseudo urgency (as in the classic, "Fax it to me"), passing the buck (e.g., "What's the point?") and so on. What follows are just a handful of the hundreds of the almost universal patterns of facile self-empowerment that not only continue to flourish but have been legitimized by the opportunistic philosophy of one-upmanship.

1. "I will definitely call you right back." There is no one I know who is not maddened, to a greater or lesser extent, by this crude but disarmingly effective maneuver which begins with the assertion that the present moment is not the appropriate time for contact. Thus the elusive other denies that he or she lacks sufficient motivation or desire to deal with whatever may be troubling the person, hinting instead that surrounding circumstances simply do not permit available time, thereby taking the matter out of their hands. It is therefore certainly not their intentions—it is the constraints of impersonal time—that is cheating the person out of the immediate attention they seem to crave.

On an unconscious level, the transaction is meant to transfer significance away from the implied, narcissistic needs of one person to the presumably more mature and worldly obligations of another. The inference is that there is a higher duty than the pressing needs of the self and this is the realm in which she is currently operating and to which she must give her allegiance. By this logic, it would be unjust to accuse her of being unequipped to meet the more personal, narcissistic needs of the caller. And compounding this, is a second complementary shift of the supposed source of interpersonal neediness: from the one who is calling to the one who is being interrupted. In effect, the other says that what is important about the interaction is the interruption it has just caused her (which, typically, would be a low priority of the person) and not the matter which motivated the caller in the first place.

By contrast, someone not invested in a power game, who is genuinely interested in what the other wants would do pretty much the reverse: indicate that what is significant is the reason for the call and that what is insignificant in the long run, but necessary in the short run (if this is really the case), is that she cannot discontinue what she is currently doing (and this is readily imparted by the sincerity with which she relays regret at being presently unavailable, but eagerness to spend time in the nearby future; and confirmed by a prompt follow-through and obvious attempt to address whatever the original issue had been).

2. "What's up?" The power of these two little words, when deftly timed, to minimize the impact of whatever the other might say or do can be remarkable. By simply reacting as though one is expecting something lighthearted in mood, superficial in content or simplistic in form to unfold is to implicitly deny that there could be anything serious going on in the transaction. That in itself can have a decidedly negative impact on the other who rightly takes it as a refusal to relate to the gravity of what he intends to express, thereby throwing him into an immediate quandary: are the needs to be articulated really as inconsequential as can be inferred from the response or has the manner in which they are being introduced surprisingly ineffective? A dynamic is thus enacted, the effect of which is to create an immediate disjunction between two parties who both know they are heading on separate relational tracks.

Variations of this strategy of unconsciously sabotaging the other through trivializing them are:

By contrast, to act as though the matter is indeed serious, but that the other's attitude or relationship to it is not.

To act as though one is well aware of the other's state of mind, but cannot understand why anyone could get worked up in the slightest over such a thing (a favorite tactic for dismissing politicians, political issues, topical events or people one does not like). The dynamic here is the same: the person denies that a need to trivialize is at the heart of what he is doing, asserting instead that it is a mere case of differing subjectivities, points of view, and states of mind. This can be an almost failsafe defense. To challenge it you have to not only suggest, but endeavor to prove that the person is being devious rather than innocently different. And to do that you have also to show that you know this person's subjective state of mind well enough to be able to penetrate to the underlying secret intention to be devaluing. Finally, compounding matters is the fact that the intent to trivialize is often presented in characteristically winsome fashion, making it difficult to challenge without being thereby painted with the same brush: i.e., it becomes easy to appear suspiciously serious if one takes issues with another's lightheartedness.

Taking a different tack, but actually the opposite side of the same coin, the person may freely acknowledge that they are in a frivolous mood that cannot do justice to the other's more somber state of mind, while insisting they have a perfect right to feel the way they happen to feel. Once again the intent to trivialize is denied, and one's irreverence to the other is portrayed as being only a symptom of the mood one is in. By this logic, for the other to protest is to thereby be cast in the role of the mood police, someone who is intrusively trying to orchestrate the expression of one's true self.

3. "What can you do?" In a typical scenario someone presents a particularly daunting piece of bad luck such as being unexpectedly fired from a job, abandoned by a lover, stabbed in the back by a friend. The auditor—unable to admit that he does not know how to empathize with the situation—pretends as though he fully understands the gravity of what is being related. On cue, in a show of good-natured stoical resignation, he, so to speak, throws up his hands, his unconscious strategy being to portray himself as someone admirably and adamantly positive-thinking, who refuses to embrace any negative event, no matter how depressing, and who can even laugh at the faces in the fact of tragedy.

4. "Why did you do that?" This is a popular and very effective strategy for making someone feel less than good about themselves. Person A acts at first as though genuinely sympathetic with the predicament that person B finds herself in. However, upon hearing that B allowed a precious opportunity to pass by for extricating herself from her situation, A snaps, "Why did you do that?" It obviously is meant to be taken as a display of well-meaning tough love. On an

unconscious level, it is an instance of pseudo empathy: unable to enter the interpersonal field of B, A feigns interest, while retreating to the safety of being an ironic critic. In turn, B senses A's unconscious refusal to empathize with her predicament, but often before B can respond, A has not surprisingly managed to change the mood or context of the exchange. The effect on B can be equivalent to a kind of psychical hit and run. On an interpersonal level, B has been lulled into experiencing a reductionism: under the guise of being presented with comprehensive, responsible feedback, she has been offered only a stereotype of her predicament.

5. "Why tell me? What do you expect me to say?" Here the trivialization is displaced from the situation and its impact on the individual who is narrating it to the relationship to the auditor, particularly to his qualifications as a confidant. The implication is that one has not earned, or does not want to earn the right to be such a confidant and that the other has either misused or misjudged the relationship to suppose otherwise. A common example of this is when someone elects to reveal a surprising sexual misadventure or secret to another who—instead of being receptively titillated, as expected—is repelled by the confession.

6. "Fax it to me." In recent years, due to its rapidly accelerating popularity, this has become an almost irresistibly easy and safe way to practice a little one-upmanship (in no small part, because it so often goes unnoted). In a typical exchange, one person approaches another with the latest information in a matter they are transacting, whereupon the other, suddenly energized, interrupts and says, "Fax it to me!" The person acts as though not only is he not avoiding, but he is so eager to work with you and get the show on the road, that nothing short of the most electronically efficient, instantaneous communication will suffice. The tone of the request is characteristically brisk and no nonsense and the latent message plainly is that time is of the essence. What is often conveniently overlooked and sometimes covered up is: that the need for a fax may have been necessitated by the fact too much time has already been squandered, that despite its state of the art credentials, it can be quite an inefficient way of communicating

if the recipient happens not to have access to a fax machine and has to seek one out, and often that much of the information to be gained by such high-tech transmission can be more simply and speedily relayed during the very time the person is requesting a fax (providing they are willing to take a little trouble). That such a person is not willing to take the required time is shown by the awkward disappointment and hesitancy which greets—perhaps the most effective counter-strategy to "fax it to me"—"Well, if you have half a minute, I can give it to you now" (the usual response being a disgruntled, "Uh...I'll get a pen").

By thus arbitrarily requesting that a fax be sent, the person identifies the work that remains to be done and shifts the burden of responsibility for doing it upon the other party. It is this other who is holding up the continuation and completion of the joint task by having been tardy or remiss in providing important information in a timely fashion. The inference is they are not really ready to be engaged in an ongoing serious dialogue. By contrast, the person—and here is where the one-upmanship comes in—has his act together and the only thing holding him up is the lack of preparation of the other.

7. "That may be a meaningful question to you, but it is not to me." This is the polite version of the much more commonplace—"What's the point?"—and it generally signals that the person is, or at least considers himself, a member of the class of intellectuals. To illustrate it, I'll give a personal anecdote. Some time ago I attended a lecture given in Manhattan by a very famous psychotherapist who happened to be one of my favorite authors. I was therefore as eager to experience his persona as listen to the paper he was scheduled to read. And I was not disappointed. The paper was predictably brilliant, his style of presentation was surprisingly charismatic and the manner in which he fielded questions from the rapt audience, when he had finished reading, was positively masterful.

The only hint of fatigue that his sterling performance might have cost him was a certain restless stirring in his chair toward the end of the Q. and A. Noticing that, I thought better of the question I was beginning to frame in my mind to put to him. But at that juncture, a woman sitting immediately in front of me rather cautiously raised her hand which, as chance would have it, caught the eye of the speaker who immediately called on her. As I remember it, her question was a friendly one, suggesting there was an obvious substantial difference between the language of a computer and the subtle discourse between therapist and patient which he had been discussing, and then asking for his comments.

To our surprise, he simply refused to do so: "Well, I don't have a computer, so while that may be a meaningful question to you, it is not to me."

Intuitively I sensed that, intentionally or not, this woman had just been dealt a real blow, one both unprovoked and unnecessary. A few minutes later, when the lecture was concluded and the crowd had dispersed, my intuition was confirmed when I accidentally encountered her in the street. No sooner had I articulated my disappointment in what I plainly regarded as the speaker's mean-spirited refusal to consider her question, than the woman—a clinical psychologist with many years experience who had long been an ardent admirer of this man--rushed to thank me, "I'm *so* glad you said that. I was beginning to wonder if I had sounded really stupid."

To reassure the woman that she hadn't, I took pains to consider and offer my interpretation of what her question had been driving at. I then went on to analyze just why I thought the speaker's short reply had been so hurtful. When I concluded by pointing out how ironic it was that a psychotherapist celebrated for his deep insights into the complexities of interpersonal relations, could be so blind when it came to the feelings of another, I could see her spirits noticeably lift.

Perhaps because the remark had been so unexpected—or rather I had expected so much more from someone presumed to be so wise in matters of the heart—the incident made a powerful impression upon me. I realized how in even the most banal and innocent of exchanges, in which one party is apparently only examining the relevance of another's question, it is possible to erode the self-worth of the other.

How is that possible? To without warning announce that one does not understand the point of what the other appears to be saying, is to thereby almost instantly stop them in their tracks. To proclaim that the listener has become lost, or is just on a different wave length, in effect is to put the responsibility on the other for reshaping their thoughts so as to make them more digestible and interesting. Beyond that there can be a latent threat: I understand well enough, but there is no substance in what you are saying and if you want me to continue to listen you are going to have to infuse more meaning and cogency into your statements.

The hidden assumption, of course, which in itself can be undermining, is that someone must always have a point to what they are saying, or that the point must very quickly become transparently clear, or that something that is merely free-associative and exploratory (like the process of psychotherapy) is thereby doomed to be interpersonally inferior to something that is informationally relevant and clear-cut. A further assumption, therefore, is that it is the auditor who knows (and not you) when you are making your point and when you are not.

From this standpoint, the maneuver of challenging the substantiveness of what the other is expressing can change the quality of the interaction from one in which there is the possibility of reciprocity to one where a unilateral demand has been issued—to make more literal sense—with the only basic question now remaining being whether or not to meet it, and how to deal with it. Thus can a seemingly innocuous demand fantastically narrow the range of relational options.

To implicitly pressure the other in this way to reframe what they are saying is an example of what I have termed *narcissistic giving* (Alper, 1996): this can be defined as a ploy which occurs when a person unconsciously wishes to deny, cover up and defend against an underlying sense that he has nothing of real value to give by acting as though he is not only giving more than enough, but is in fact giving grandiosely. Part of its pattern is to take what is really a crumb (in terms of true nurturance) and by treating it as though it were a gratuity, to thereby achieve the secondary gain of not having to work on the hidden deficit and conflict over giving. In the present instance, someone acknowledges on the one hand that the subjective investment of meaning is a primary ingredient in a mutually enhancing interaction, but asserts on the other hand that it is just this subjective investment of meaning that is so lacking or disjunctive on the issue in question, that nothing fruitful can currently come of it.

The implication is that the person is thoroughly available for a meaningful, nurturing, reciprocal interchange but that the minimal conditions for its implementation are absent. Furthermore, by first talking about what is meaningful to the other, the inference is that this is how he approaches interactions: he has an eye on what is or is not worth investing in.

But, of course, it is the reverse that is true. The person we are describing is narcissistically interested in what only has meaning for himself. This is shown by how quickly he appears ready to give up on either further exploring a possible, secondary connotation of a question which—although it did not initially stimulate him—might subsequently prove mutually engaging, or (if not) searching for a likely link to a common interest.

It should be noted this can almost always be accomplished. A teacher that is merely interested in appealing questions is scarcely a teacher. A certain significance can always be lent to a sterile question or interaction simply by pointing out in a nurturing way what the person finds lacking. He or she thereby offers to *share* meaning. Thus, in our example, had the lecturer been so-minded he could have, without compromising his own ideas, replied, "I am having trouble relating to your analogy to computer language because I happen to feel ..." In short—for someone to honestly articulate the obstacles they experience which make it difficult to find meaning in what the other is saying—is to reveal a differing point of view that in itself can become more stimulating than a straightforward, informational answer.

But, again, it is just this the person cannot do and under cover of pseudo intellectualism he therefore attacks the question and rejects the interrogator as being unworthy of a response.

By contrast, in what might be termed the *dynamics of nurturance*, we see someone who:

Not only accepts, but actively searches for the area of developmental deprivation, which he or she then seeks to cultivate. For such an individual satisfaction comes not from immediate gratification but from an ability to actualize the potential and be a facilitator of the attainment of enhanced personal meaning for the other. The one who is therefore intent on nurturing—instead of using a perception of a developmental lag between self and other as a justification for abandoning the relationship—becomes motivated to get involved.

Because of this, a person who chooses to nurture a relationship will often not feel deprived by a perceived inequity (provided it is not too great) in the ability to give. An obvious reason for this will be that the nurturer—who dynamically will tend not to feel needy—may not be threatened by the lack of any immediate prospects for being reciprocally nourished. On the contrary, he or she is likely to maintain an attitude of hope. After all, based on past successes, there is reason to believe the disparity in giving that presently exists can be compensated for by the apparent excess of healthy narcissistic supplies that the nurturer has in readiness. Thus, the act of nurturance tends to be grounded in optimism: the inability of the other to reciprocate is not due to irreversible arrest but may represent an insufficient contact with a facilitating environment (an unconscious belief which echoes the professional credo of the Kohutian self psychologist, 1971—that is, by nurturing you do more than provide what is manifestly needed, you begin to make reparation for the failure of parental figures in the past to be appropriately empathic).

Not surprisingly, the aim to achieve one-upmanship over the other, from the standpoint of intimacy, is the antithesis of the intent to nurture. In each instance, the strategy is to trivialize, to keep searching the interpersonal context for exploitable signs of superficiality or weakness. The basic ploy is to put the other on the defensive while calling attention to their somber, alarmed or needy state of mind, the undermining inference being that it is the person's failure to adapt, defend or adequately master that is at the root of the designated problem.

NEGATIVE CLOSURE

Typically, this occurs when someone who is in a position, if so-minded, to facilitate another's request—say to accept an application, to provide some necessary information, to render a service—not only declines to cooperate but presents their decision (that affects two people) as a fait accompli, something no longer to be considered. The other is thus included in the process only in the sense of being apprised of something he or she needs to know: i.e., that the matter has been settled. The implication is that the other was incapable, not needed or not entitled to participate in the actual decision-making.

Such a person therefore acts as though the only thing at stake is the carrying out of her autonomous decision. In itself this is quite intimidating to the other because now to protest can be taken as an encroachment upon the person's autonomy. It is left for the other to either fall in line, and thereby swallow a dismissal, or speak up and risk what is likely to be a tense confrontation.

Someone who practices negative closure adopts a strategy or course of action that is likely to have a decidedly adverse impact on the other but presents it as though an equitable resolution for both parties has just been reached. It is particularly galling to the recipient because it produces almost the opposite effect: unrest, emotional disturbance, a sense of mistrust and lack of understanding that resists being put to rest (they are being asked not only to suppress the needs of their true self but to collude in the acceptance of something that is inimical to their best interests).

Negative closure is therefore threatening because it seems to imply that clarity has been arrived at, a clarity, moreover, that has at its center the perception of something that is wrong with you. Clarity, itself, is threatening because it suggests that the ego is undivided in its judgment and that, therefore, whatever course of action it adopts will not be impeded by inner dissension. As a result, its expression tends to be characterized by a certain forcefulness—befitting an apparent resolute messenger from the core of the self—that makes it difficult to combat (because whenever the true self reveals itself one wants—even if one disagrees with its perspective—to engage, rather than contend with it).

It follows the seeming clarity of negative closure puts the other in a double bind: on the one hand he is drawn to defer to the authoritativeness of the act, but on the other, he is perhaps equally compelled to contest the blatant non-reciprocity. By contrast, interpersonal closure requires mutuality, and this is especially so if the intention of one party—howsoever reluctantly—is to withdraw narcissistic supplies, be punitive or close off a prior avenue of interaction (the flip side of this coin, of course, is what might be called premature positive closure—the case when someone who is satisfied beyond their expectations, decides to take the goodies and run).

Examples:

1. "I don't want to talk about this anymore." This is perhaps the most common instance of negative closure and is almost a fail-safe rejection. The announcement, which typically is delivered in the course of an ongoing, heated disagreement, abruptly leaves the other stranded, but acts as though the real issue is that the person is feeling oppressed by the intensity of the argument. It is implied that any attempt to protest the unfairness of such arbitrary closure—by pointing out the issue is still unresolved and that to nip the discussion in the bud is to place the other in a state of deprivation—is seemingly to disrespect the person's autonomous right not to talk about what he or she chooses not to. And while the other may feel his need to talk is as valid and important to him as the person's need not to, it is nevertheless difficult to press the point, assertively trying to keep the conversation going, without seeming aggressive in an offensive way. To put it another way, from the standpoint of the one who is being conversationally left hanging, the person—rather than true autonomy—is showing pseudo-independence: under the pretense of choosing to keep their own counsel, they are hiding their need to withdraw from an interpersonal field of legitimate and unresolved conflict.

2. "My feelings for you have changed." This unilateral act of rejection—the famous prelude to the announcement that the romance is over—may be the most potent example of interpersonal negative closure. What is being terminated is nothing less than the relationship to the self. The realization to the rejectee that the decision on whether or not to go on seeing one another has in one fell swoop been taken completely out of his hands, is unbearably painful and emasculating.

Here it is seen just how the toxicity of not only rejection, but all kinds of abusive treatment of the other, can masquerade as the right of the self to act autonomously. Autonomy, with its culturally loaded approval for instances of so-called self-actualization, can thereby serve as a defense and cover for a hostile misuse of the other. Since manifest aggression can equally be either on behalf of the person or against the other, the issue becomes one of intentionality: always a tough case to prove. The person—claiming only he can know his own motives—can insist, if challenged, that he is merely asserting his own rights rather than violating those of another.

For all of these reasons, anyone at any time is free to reject anyone else. But rejection is frightening because insidiously it transforms interpersonal issues of process and feeling into exercises of will power (see Leslie Farber for a brilliant examination of the pernicious "Ways of the Will", 1966). Rejection is the example par excellence of negative closure inasmuch as it attempts to arbitrarily freeze a process that is in flux, organic and to a large extent unconscious (the antithesis of positive closure which usually follows upon completion of a genuinely autonomous task or provides needed relief from an emotional turbulence—e.g., going to a friend's funeral). Rejection—which is often experienced as someone passing a judgment, a sentence of doom on what was thought to be a viable relationship—can thereby feel like a psychic abortion, the imposition of an alien will, the ultimate anti-empathic presence.

Indeed, rejection typically is perceived as being so anti-empathic that it is hard not to believe—despite the disclaimers that are usually handed out, "It's not you, it's me" ... "You wouldn't be happy if we continued together"—that the person has come to truly hate you. And, ironically, the very fact that the rejector is going to some trouble to deny this can seem to confirm the impression of being despised—the person being too shameless to even confess that he or she has obviously inflicted considerable harm on the other.

BEING IMPOSSIBLE

Patients in psychotherapy report and complain of an almost infinite variety of real or imagined narcissistic injuries from which they presumably suffer. One of the most obvious and glaring offenders (referred to, in a different context, by Christopher Bollas, 1993, as a "cute monster") is the individual who seemingly thrives on being impossible. Such a person may, without thinking twice about it, disdain to return phone calls, pay back debts, keep promises, honor obligations or, in general, manifest even a minimal concern for the feelings or sensibilities of the other. If they happen to be involved in a close or familial relationship with another, they are likely to behave in such a consistently outrageous fashion that the other is forced to either totally abandon them or try to laugh off and thereby deny their antics. What follows--since this kind of behavior is fertile soil for the growth of power games--is a profile, culled from many examples, of the impossible person:

Perhaps foremost is that being impossible is self-parodying. It puts its own behavior in question so that the perpetrator, in effect, if called to accountability, will have some ready-made disclaimers: for example, that he obviously doesn't really mean what he seems to be saying and doing because he would have to be awfully stupid not to recognize he is often over the top: that he is only, as is his nature, acting theatrically and hyperbolically; that his behavior is actually a cry for help since he must be very upset to be so overreacting; that he would not be driven to such desperate measures for soliciting attention unless he was not getting through, not being listened to; that he must truly care about, even if he is overstating what he is saying, otherwise he would not be going to fantastic lengths to dramatize it; that if his actions were just smoke and mirrors, the other would not be upset, too, which proves there is at least something to be taken seriously; and so on.

It immediately becomes apparent that acting outrageously can offer—in addition to defenses—some handy accusations to counter the other's predictable complaints: that is, if they weren't being provoked in the first place, they wouldn't overreact; if the other understood what their needs were and could be more giving, they would no doubt be considerably more satisfied and hence more restrained; they behave in the wretched way they do because they have lost hope in the relationship so that the real underlying agent of the present chaos is the other who has rejected and demoralized them.

Parodying conventional behavior can suggest that the world itself is absurd, that one therefore cannot help finding oneself in zany and soap opera-like situations, and that that is the true problem and not the actions of the person caught in the system. From that standpoint, what one does is a reflecting mirror of the madness of the surrounding world. What is more, there could be an unconscious strategy of alarming and thereby diverting the other by challenging their expectations of an orderly, interpersonal world—by breaking up habitual psychic links (Bion, 1967)—and forcing them, to the extent they are disoriented, to endeavor, if only internally, to reestablish their private philosophy of life. Since someone has to keep the chaos from escalating, the other—who obviously cannot trust the holding function of the person who is behaving impossibly—is induced into becoming an involuntary container.

It follows the individual who acts outrageously passes along an inner turbulence for another's processing. If the other cannot process it, she in turn is in danger of being contained or swallowed up. It is significant the recipient is coerced into reacting and not allowed simply to be. The capacity for creative reverie (what Christopher Bollas, 1987, has referred to as evocativeness) is drastically curtailed. Outrageous behavior—by cornering the other and presenting only the option of relating to its disturbing effects—can thereby seem bigger than the self. Indeed, it can suggest that the self of the one who is being impossible is but a symptom at the mercy of an underlying elemental force. In that sense, it is a way to appear charismatic without actually having the concentrated psychic charge that denotes the genuinely charismatic personality (compensating for lack of quality with quantity).

By shoving one relationally off balance, the impossible person makes the interpersonal homeostasis that normally is taken for granted the primary issue. The other is forced to attempt to regain their lost composure. An almost intolerable surcharge of tension is created that causes everything else to pale next to the self-evident necessity of reducing it.

A mystery is thereby evoked in the spectator who, sooner or later, is spellbound by the unrelenting drama of the person's antics. Interrelating is unconsciously deferred until the storm passes (which may take years). By driving the spectator back, the impossible person creates the space that he needs.

The other, reduced to an audience, is perplexed. Since the person is so obviously overreacting, and cannot be simply responding to the immediate situation, unacknowledged, hidden factors must be in operation. In an effort to understand, so as to perhaps better manage an imminent crisis, the other cannot help but speculate as to the true genesis of the present turmoil. By contrast, the person who externalizes and projectively identifies with certain intolerable tensions that have been placed in another, may achieve a measure of relief. By acting outrageously, someone may feel that not only are they being honest by letting it all hang out, but that they are also showing courage by allowing the chips to fall where they may. They may feel that, by bringing things to a head, they are thereby on the brink of closure, that they are simultaneously protecting themselves by providing a cover—via the emotional disturbance they are brewing—so that, whenever necessary, they can retreat into themselves without appreciable resistance or notice. That no matter how upset they may be making the other, at least no one can accuse them of being boring. And that finally, regardless of what their point may be, there is little danger they are not making it and even less so that it will be easily forgotten.

For all of these reasons, to be impossible, from a psychoanalytic point of view, is to unconsciously transform a potentiality for collaborative interrelating into a state of suspense: one waits to see how the drama that is unfolding will turn out. Insidiously, the relationship becomes plot-driven and crisis-driven. Outrageous behavior fills an interpersonal void that would be otherwise gaping. It guarantees there can to no ordinary progression of the interaction. Instead, it brings things to a dead halt, what Christopher Bollas (1995)—in speaking of obsessional repetitiveness—has referred to as "a terminal object". Now the goal is simply to contain the turbulence and, except for fantasies of subsequent relief or escape, there is no sense of what to do with the person.

Typically, the unconscious strategy of the unwilling spectator is to locate where the madness is: in situational factors beyond the control of the perpetrator, which are driving him to the wall; or in the core of the person, in psychic forces, which no longer willing to be suppressed, are finally being unleashed? So the first question becomes—is the person the agent or the target of his own irrationality? Is he a conduit or a manufacturer of turbulence? And the second question is— what is the other's relation to the chaos going to be? As a mesmerized, although helpless, frightened spectator? Or is the other meant to be a conduit also, to empathically share in the madness?

Being outrageous and impossible immediately makes what would otherwise be a routine response problematical. Any possible relationship now must to be to the behavior as symptom and not to the self. The other is thereby denied the comfort of customary, trusted responses and forced to improvise. By rendering irrelevant most of the habitual reactions of the other which are based on a sane, orderly social universe, a level playing field of sorts can be created with someone who ordinarily is perceived as holding the upper hand. By creating an unmanageable surplus of emotion, it breaks the normal feedback loop: reaction tends instead to be to the aftermath—the field of tension engendered by the disruptive behavior—and not to the underlying expressive self. By painting the other into a corner and forcing her to respond to what are essentially centrifugal emotions, psychic side effects, to be impossible is also to play an effective power game.

BEING CRITICAL

Typically, undiluted, pointed criticism has a stun gun effect: it instantaneously, if momentarily, immobilizes its victim; forcing him to adopt a defensive posture—one of the most popular of which is to deny that one has been affected by the criticism.

Unlike the person who wrongfully accuses another, the critic comports himself as though he is not out to get anyone or to correct an injustice; he is instead merely commenting on a common human foible. The critic almost always denies that the criticism is a subjective expression of a negative or hostile intention. Whenever his criticism is attacked for being perhaps excessively zealous, his classic rejoinder tends to be: "You're taking this personally," ... "You're too thin-skinned," ... "You don't have a sense of humor." The very most the critic is likely to admit is that his remarks—while perhaps not sensitively or constructively construed—inasmuch as they represent how he honestly feels, have an authenticity that needs to be articulated.

Everyday, interpersonal criticism is usually presented as being in the service of carrying on the relationship in an unguarded, forthright manner. From this point of view, the critic is obliged to unburden himself. Not to speak what is on his mind, would feel stifling. To therefore take offense at, and question his right to say what he is saying is to disrespect his need for autonomous self-expression.

For all of these reasons, someone who is strongly and unselfconsciously critical of another typically sets off two powerful denials: first, that the criticism itself was harshly intended or in any way mean-spirited and second, that the recipient—other than perhaps being annoyed at what she may consider an unjust reproach—was personally affected by something she cannot in good faith take seriously. (Of course, what makes this latter defense hard to maintain, is that criticism that really is hostilely conceived will often take dead aim at that which is blatantly true: unconsciously, no doubt because it perceives that it will carry more weight, register a greater impact and be that much harder to deflect or ignore).

It follows that to be critical is to immediately thrust the other into a position of having to do unwanted, but necessary psychic work: she has to fend off whatever is perceived as the toxic impact of the criticism—most often by denying it—while simultaneously managing to present a facade of passable self-confidence. To do this she has to, first, cover up that she has just lost her composure; second, regain her composure; and, third, to camouflage the usually intense effort, which would be a giveaway, that this typically requires.

Once, however, she has done this psychic work, more or less to her satisfaction—so that she feels safe to go on the offensive—she may begin to consider how to pay back her unsolicited critic. There are a number of ways of doing this. The most common is to return the favor--but secretly: she in turn critically reevaluates the preexisting relationship on the basis of the toxic criticism just received, and, not surprisingly, finds it decidedly unsatisfying. There is then an inevitable loss of trust in someone who can be so unfairly judgmental. She may then blame herself for trusting such a person in the first place and attribute her gullibility to the fact that, obviously she did not see the criticism coming. (It is part of the dynamic of the act of being critical, and why it has the impact it does, that the target—regardless of the warning signs, of how often she may have been criticized in the past—is more or less shocked by its occurrence. Another way to say this, is that there seems to be in all of us a built-in, self-protective denial that such things could happen (allowing us to socialize as intrepidly as we do).

Once someone has been critically wounded, however, all social bets are off and the person—to insure that the offense is not repeated—will begin, to a greater or lesser extent, to withdraw from the relationship. But there is no point in telling this to the other. It would, after all, take considerable trust to reveal that one not only has just suffered a narcissistic injury by what has been said, but, as a result, needs to distance herself.

Instead the counter criticism becomes covert and thereby enjoys several immediate advantages: it is safe because it cannot be deflected, or discredited if it is unknown to the other; it is powerful because it plainly is holding the key to the future of the relationship, yet is exclusively in the ownership of only one person. She will therefore conceal the fact that the basis for the lack of interrelating is the narcissistic injury she has incurred in the hope that her new, deliberately diffident posture may seem to be a natural evolution and expression of how she has come to view the other (so as to be that much more of a devastating rebuke). In other words, in a perverse mirror reaction, she wants her intensive reactive animosity to the one who has undeniably hurt her to pass for an unbiased, non-defensive and seemingly objective point of view. Finally, there is a sense in which she has been unconsciously disillusioned—not only by the other—but by the truth or what is supposed to be the critical faculty of the human mind: i.e., if that is all the other thinks of her despite everything she's done, then perhaps there is something defective about psychical perception itself, something not worth pursuing. (The denial that one has been injured by the criticism is used to thwart the relevance of the other's supposed objectivity—the chief impact of which, after all, has been to belittle the person).

What happens, now, imperceptibly, is that both parties begin to play an interpersonal role, each pretending that the humiliating undertones of the critical remarks were not intended and not heard. It amounts to *as if interrelating*: to make it work, each has to collude in the fiction of the other's role as well as their own, not unlike two actors both acting and reacting to one another.

The irony, however, is that psychic energy is then diverted into being real in imaginary circumstances (the well-known actor's credo), instead of—as is characteristic of the enactment of genuine intimacy—being real in real circumstances.

BEING ANXIOUS

Ralph, a patient I had been seeing for several years, is startled shortly after his fiftieth birthday when his internist, Dr. Maisey, a man whom he trusts greatly, suggests that the time has arrived to have a colonoscopy. A colonoscopy, Ralph informs me in case I didn't know, is a procedure whereby a long tube affixed to a miniature camera is inserted in the rectum, and then guided through the lower colon, all along the large intestine and then back out. A major purpose is to ascertain the absence or presence of colon cancer, the likelihood of which increases after the age of fifty. It is a procedure, according to Ralph's mother and older brother—who both speak from experience—that is unbearably uncomfortable (e.g., "You don't want to know about it").

It is obvious to Ralph, who has been taking medication for mild hypertension for the past ten years, that at the very least he will be facing a considerable ordeal that he can only hope does not live up to its depressing billing. He is glad that the surgical procedure, to be performed in the outpatient endoscopy wing of St. Vincent's Hospital has been scheduled for the following month. There will be time and sessions in which to tackle his unavoidable anxiety.

And in the weeks to come, Ralph, true to his prediction, is flooded with apprehension. His anxiety takes shape in the form of interminable questions. What are the degrees of severity of colon cancer and the probability of its occurrence? To what extent is it treatable? How often is it curable? When is it and when is it not operable? If necessary, how major is the operation considered?

One notable feature of his anxiety was that he did not pursue, indeed could not bear finding out any of the answers to these questions. It was as though by voicing his worst fears, by acknowledging there was a need to confront them, he had done all that could be reasonably required of him. It was enough to name them and then do his best to put them out of his mind.

In this Ralph is relatively successful, up until about three days before the scheduled procedure, when his anxiety returns with a vengeance. At work, he is so preoccupied that he can think of little else. Although he is leery of taking the golighty—the gallon of emetic that he is instructed to slowly drink over a four hour period twenty four hours prior to his admission, and which is needed to cleanse the large intestine and colon—in a weird way, he is relieved to at last be able to fixate on a specified task, albeit a nausea-producing one. And while he repeatedly gags and is on the verge of throwing up many times, he manages, doggedly, to down the golighty.

On the day of the procedure, Ralph is accompanied by his girlfriend, Carolyn, with whom he has been living for five years. On the prep sheet which he dutifully followed to the letter, he was advised to bring someone—in case he was dizzy—to escort him home after the procedure. Had he not been so advised, he would have brought Carolyn anyway, for he was painfully aware that he was in desperate need of moral support.

To provide some sense and flavor of his extraordinary state of anxiety, here is Ralph's own account of his traumatic experience:

"I arrived at the clinic soon after it opened, with Carolyn. Within minutes after checking in with the receptionist, Dr. Maisey emerged from a back corridor. I thought he seemed nervous when I introduced him for the first time to my girlfriend. He gave me a pen, handed me some forms and joked, 'Here. You have to sign your life away.' I signed without even attempting to read a single word. I was already much too anxious to think about the consent that I was giving in the event of certain complications. I do remember Dr. Maisey, doing his duty, telling me a month ago that the procedure is safe. 'The only thing that can go wrong is it can puncture the colon, in which case you'd have to be immediately hospitalized. But that's never happened to me.'

"I could feel myself getting more anxious by the second, so I tried to strike up a soothing conversation with Carolyn, but a nurse appeared and very nicely asked me to follow her. It meant something to me that she seemed genuinely concerned about how I was and almost immediately I began to like her. I was more than ready to put myself in her hands and eager to do whatever she asked me. When she led me to a small dressing room, handed me a dressing gown and a key to a locker in which to hang my clothes, my first thought was to change as quickly as possible so as to please her. And when I had trouble fastening the two gown strings behind my back, being klutzy as usual, my main worry was that she would lose respect for me.

"But she was a colonoscopy nurse, that's all she did all day long, she later told me, and I guess she was very used to people being nervous. The more anxious I became, the calmer, friendlier and more comforting she was. By the time I got to the room in which the procedure was going to be done, I was wondering if I had a tiny crush on her. At least it took my mind off what was about to happen.

"Dr. Maisey was waiting for me and he was all business. He told me in advance each thing he was about to do. First was the injection of a sedative to relax me during the procedure. I liked the idea of that. Then he took my blood pressure: an astonishingly and dangerously high 193 over 137, by far the highest reading in my life. Dr. Maisey shook his head—as though to say it's like you to react like that to a procedure like this—and laughed ruefully. Not to worry, the sedative will bring it down. The nurse handed me a thin tube connected to a tank that was blowing oxygen through air holes into my nostrils. I was told to lie on my side on a narrow table. I was already beginning to feel drowsy. Dr. Maisy announced he was going to insert the tube with the tiny camera in my rectum. As he did so, he cautioned there might be an uncomfortable, cramped sensation. It didn't feel too bad at all.

"Dr. Maisey was standing behind me, with the nurse by his side as he slowly worked the tube up my rectum. I noticed that every few seconds he would look up and stare at a monitor mounted on a wall to my left. It took me a little while to realize that the monitor was a kind of television set and that the strange, kaleidoscopic lights, shapes and shadows were actual moving pictures of the insides of my colon and large intestine, recorded by the probing, miniature camera.

"Rather childishly, I asked Dr. Maisey whether I should look at the monitor. I wanted to be told what to do, to be taken care of. 'If you want to,' he said, not taking his eyes off the screen. Perhaps because I wanted to, I interpreted that as encouragement to look. By now I estimated the camera had entered my large intestine. Increasingly, I was morbidly fascinated by this televised medical exploration of my bowels.

"I was too terrified to inquire—as I watched the monitor—what the signs of cancer looked like. Were they instantly recognizable, something you knew when you saw it, even if you were an untrained novice such as myself? Or were they subtle, revealing themselves only to the practiced eye of a medical detective, which means they might already have been spotted? But if that were the case, wouldn't, shouldn't they have told me?

"When the nurse, as though reading my mind, cheerfully reported, 'You're doing great. Just a little bit more," I was hugely relieved, as though my life had just been saved. I felt the tube come out and knew the procedure was over. The nurse removed the oxygen tube from my nose, helped me off the table and began escorting me down a corridor to the locker that had my clothes. I was surprised how wobbly my legs seemed and at one point I slightly tripped. Laughing and grabbing my arm the nurse said, 'Be careful. You did so well in there, it would be a shame if something happened to you out here.' She was really sweet.

"When I saw Carolyn waiting for me in the recovery room I couldn't have been happier. Someone gave me orange juice and crackers. A few minutes later, somebody else took my blood pressure and it was normal. Finally, Dr. Maisey came by and told me everything was fine. He doesn't feel comfortable whenever I express gratitude for his help, but I did it anyway."

After Ralph had finished recounting in graphic detail his traumatic experience I asked him if, other than that he had turned fifty, there had been any reason to suspect that the colonoscopy might show that he had colon cancer. Ralph was emphatic: "I asked Dr. Maisey that. He said there was no history of colon cancer in my family, so there was no reason to think that."

Ralph's extreme overreaction had afforded me an opportunity to study the vicissitudes of an anxiety attack. The final stage—after the anxiety had dissipated—was especially interesting. When the colonoscopy had revealed not a trace of colon cancer, Ralph had experienced a serendipitous euphoria of relief, as though he had been granted a genuine second chance at life. It is a euphoria, however, that quickly wears off once you are reunited with your pre-anxious self: at which point all the daily fears—which had been effectively suppressed—come clamoring back and you are surprised at how seriously you again take concerns which by comparison can only seem petty. This may be explained by the fact that the person has sustained a twofold narcissistic injury: the loss of euphoria and the return of recently suppressed anxieties.

From an interpersonal standpoint, someone who is anxious relates differently. Since, on the one hand they are more needy and demanding of attention, but on the other, feel unworthy of being helped—they are especially sensitive to any perceived rebuff. This became especially clear—as was the case with Ralph—in his relationship to his doctor. At such times patients are made aware of a painful truth: that doctors, when they are called upon but are unable to relate, will often resort to infantilizing their patients, unconsciously insisting that instruction, which can be controlled, and not empathy, which cannot, is what is required. And the empathy that is dispensed tends to be done so in an almost perversely trivializing way: thus Dr. Maisey—who merely tried to laugh off the dangerously high blood pressure reading of his patient—seemed at pains to inform Ralph that he might feel a sting as the tube began to be inserted in his rectum, but he neglected to tell him, as Ralph would subsequently complain, that the gallon of golighty he would be imbibing the day prior to the colonoscopy would be one of the most physically nauseating experiences of his life. On the contrary, on the hospital prep sheet instructing him how and when to drink the golighty, the only caveat was "if you feel nauseous, you may stop..." (This is analogous to the standard safety instructions with demonstrations by stewardesses on airplanes: a situation—that, should it occur, would undoubtedly precipitate mass panic—is described with absurd tranquillity. The unconscious strategy being that everything that might require an open-ended, on-the-spot, relational and empathic response, everything, that is, that cannot be predicted and calibrated in advance—is to be denied. In short, when relating is reduced to the dispensing of canned information, as is the case with airline stewardesses' safety instructions and most physician-patient consultations, then the covert agenda is to be able to foretell the future and not experience it.)

To return to Ralph. His level of anxiety had been so extraordinary—for an admittedly stressful, although routine procedure—that I could only wonder how he would have reacted had there been real cause for concern. Because his responses were so extreme and vivid, they provided me with a kind of paradigm for the dynamics of anxiety to which I now turn.

Someone who is anxious waits for one's anxiety, and part of the anxiety vis-á-vis one's anxiety is that one cannot predict its arrival and departure. All one can be sure of is that dread will be engendered. Anxiety, as an object or state of mind characteristically seems global, faceless and without a particular identity. It's well-known floating quality makes it seem less substantial than other emotions—more like a mirror of the mood of the self than about the relationship between self and object.

At various times, being anxious can feel like an inner crumbling, a loss of resolve, a puzzling inner gnawing, a subversive quicksand state, with the ground continually shifting under one's feet. More than a worry which (as Adam Phillips points out in his great essay on the subject, 1993) at least comes ready made with a rationale for being concerned, anxiety seems without foundation and to that extent a sign of weakness and indecisiveness. To be anxious means that one's insecurity and uneasiness have come to occupy the foreground. The absence of a concrete object-referent highlights the unattached affect. It is easy to grow anxious that one is anxious and anxiety can be taken as a warning that one has become dangerously vulnerable in a certain neglected area of the psyche.

For all these reasons, anxiety is demoralizing. Perhaps, of all the emotions, it does not seem to go anywhere. On the contrary, it has a scattering effect: one seems to be traveling in circles, marking time, and always returning to the original worry. The fact one cannot put one's finger on what is bothering one—the fear that does not know its name—makes one think one must have overlooked something important. Automatically, one tends to become conservative and introspective. There is the fear that one has overextended oneself.

Someone who is anxious is in the paradoxical position of searching—for the terrible chink in one's psychic armor or in the object of fear—without knowing what one is searching for. To be anxious, therefore, is to feel unintuitive, clueless and lacking in insight (in the unconscious this can be equated with psychic blindness). The realization that one is acutely afraid without the object being even in sight can easily seem as though one is literally being afraid of one's shadow. Which in itself can be both frightening and anxiety-producing. The question now becomes—not what is the underlying object one really fears—but what are the hidden gaps, the soft spots in the self that have led to the overvaluation and obsessive imaginings of the threats to one's safety? From such a perspective, one's sickly imagination is the real problem.

Inasmuch as there is always the sense of being unable to control one's fear, to be anxious is to feel like a coward. Fear therefore turns inward and someone is frightened, not so much of the external threat, but of how they will react from within. Feeling sufficiently anxious over time can seem as though they are suffering from a *disease* of fear: their ability to contain it mysteriously has begun to pathologically malfunction.

To be anxious is to be surrounded by fear. Unconsciously the situation may be equated to a kind of psychic minefield—you know there is something out there to be frightened of, but you can't locate, be sure of its source, or that there is one source. Indeed, the floating, global, field nature of anxiety makes it seem plausible there is more than a single source of fear, that there is, instead, what might be called *an atmospheric danger.*

It follows intense, sustained anxiety has an isolating and alienating effect upon the psyche. The fact that nothing apparently reassures you, that anything and everything can suggest cause for worry reinforces the idea that you are alone and have been abandoned to your doubts. The traditional reassurances that are offered—"Take it one step at a time" ... "You're making too much of it" ... "There's no point in worrying about it" ...—seem oddly irrelevant—inasmuch as they are typically couched in common-sense, rational-emotive, cognitive tips—and do not even try to address the eerie, blatantly irrational fear that is enveloping one.

To the person who is anxious, who is aware he can no longer think and emotionally react in an apparently rational manner, it is difficult to justify to himself the almost pervasive alarm to which he feels susceptible. It is as though, when in this state, he has lot his normal capacity to proceed in a linear way to master the obstacles he is encountering and at such times is decidedly not himself. A basic defense, therefore, when anxious, is simply to slow down, calm down and seek to restore oneself by getting back and reconnecting to one's pre-anxious self. And since one often feels, when anxious, that one is acting out of an irrational and childlike part of the self, one almost automatically tires to coax oneself back to adulthood by activating one's internalized exhortative parental voice: e.g., "There's nothing to be upset about" ... "Don't make a mountain out of a molehill" ... "You have to, and can face up to whatever is bothering you". In short, one calls upon one's inner parent to cajole and reprimand oneself, as a reminder that one after all is a tried and tested adult with a functioning and decision-making mind.

For all of these reasons, someone who is anxious may be mystified at their inability to cope with what to others is only an ordinary environment. He or she may believe that what is needed is to disengage from whatever is upsetting their equilibrium. They may sense that the more they try, the less they accomplish. They may resort to a meditative retreat: one searches to reestablish an underlying psychic symmetry that seems to have been broken. Invariably, to a greater or lesser extent, anxiety, as a state of mind, feels meaningless: the ultimate blind alley.

What are some other defenses, in addition to attempting to calm oneself down, against such an unwelcome psychic constellation? Perhaps foremost is the ritualistic propitiation—by dint of repetitive worries—to a malign, felt presence that, in its unknowability, can feel uncanny. Inasmuch as persistent anxiety feels like pressure, and pressure like punishment, the person may unconsciously and guiltily conclude that he is suffering retribution for something he has failed to do or take care of. There may therefore be a moralistic quality to his obsessive attempts at self-protection: "See, I am doing all I can to resolve whatever is wrong (so stop criticizing and persecuting me)."

A second and very common defense is denial. By acting as though what needs to be done or attended to is comprised of comparatively small, repetitive details, one denies that whatever is bothering the person—which has continued to so disrupt and monopolize the ordinary stream of consciousness—is significant. (On the contrary, it is exactly the type of thing that cannot be resolved with tiny, mechanical, reparative steps). And a corollary phase of such denial—that the primary cause of anxiety can be safely managed by obsessive compartmentalization—is the self-deception that one is thereby not only responding to but dynamically interacting with whatever is causing the problem. In effect, this might be called *the black box theory* of anxiety: it is not necessary to know what one fears, it is only necessary to take enough preventive steps and plug every conceivable loophole so as to hem in whatever one is afraid of. Sooner or later, according to this unconscious strategy—if one casts a wide enough net—one will hit on the right means with which to combat the enemy.

It follows that part of this desire to propitiate is to respond immediately to any hint of worry. Someone who is anxious acts obsequiously towards his fear. But this creates a double bind: one is too insecure and demoralized to stick with any single course of action, but too frightened to do nothing. Anxious behavior can then be viewed as a defense based on perpetual motion: on being a moving target, hard to hit and afraid to slow down. By spreading himself thin the anxious person creates the illusion—that by having a full agenda of things to worry about—one will not have time to meet up with a particular, truly daunting, and demanding fear. His aim, so to speak, is to lose himself in a *crowd of fears*. His unconscious wish is that whatever he is really frightened of shall remain anonymous. His desire is not to have an intimate relationship with his fears, not to have to get to really know them. Being anxious, therefore, can be a way of being safely promiscuous with one's fears. It follows, as an internal object relation, someone who is anxious primarily relates to what he doubts, worries and fears. The relationship is to what he might see or encounter—to a dreaded future rather than to a threatening present, to a what if rather than a what is.

When this is so, as was the case with my patient, Ralph, anxiety will manifest itself as an obsessive concern with something that the person cannot, but would like to avert. A state of anxiety is then experienced as a foretaste of a charged encounter with a fated event—a scheduled operation, the result of a biopsy, a determination by a boss as to whether one will be fired or retained at one's job, a decision from a lover as to whether to continue or break off a relationship—in which a great deal is hanging in the balance but in which the person feels he or she has little say. Because the participant perceives the outcome of the critical event to depend on factors largely out of his control, it is natural for his anxiety to focus on antecedent small, manageable steps.

As the date of the event approaches, however, it will become increasingly difficult—inasmuch one believes one is going to be faced with a massive threat—to contain one's fear through the strategy of ritualistic compartmentalization. Indeed, when fear cannot march forward or proceed to action, or be envisioned as at least translatable into action—in other words when fear feels helpless—it engenders anxiety. This is another way of saying when fear loses its grip on its chosen object, and in a panicky way begins to search for a reassuring substitute, it is transformed into and experienced as anxiety. Anxiety is then both the process and outcome of a desperate search for a plausible object to ground it: something it can safely fear.

Of course, fear rarely stands by itself, there usually being at least some anxiety about whatever it is one is afraid of (in this regard, see Adam Phillips brilliant discussion and question—Is fear the truth of anxiety or is anxiety the truth of fear?—in his *Terrors and Experts*, 1995). Anxiety can be differentiated from fear by its lack of simple-minded specificity. By contrast, it is as though one is fighting an opponent—the outline of which, including a number of features, one can see very well—but which one suspects has hidden parts (and about which one cannot stop worrying). This leads us to the following formula: worry plus uncertainty equals anxiety.

If someone has, for example, lost his keys, he may fear he may never find them. If, on the other hand, someone senses he has mislaid or forgotten something important but can't put his finger on it, he may become anxious. Of course, this difference, as mentioned, is too neat and one not only fears but becomes exceedingly anxious that one may not find one's keys.

To the extent that fear turns into anxiety, it is anxiety that seems to occupy the foreground of one's consciousness. The impact is twofold. There are present fears and there are unknown fears linked somehow to the conscious fear (a connection one intuits but cannot discern). The anxiety, therefore, may be likened to a psychic iceberg: one is terrified of the tip—for example, finding out that one has colon cancer—because one knows how dangerous that is, but one really fears what is beneath the water and cannot be seen (what it really means and feels like to live as a cancer patient). The dynamic may be something like this: fear of something initiates defensive, action-oriented thoughts, feelings and behavior, but the subsequent anxious perception that there are far too many aspects of the anticipated situation to be seen and comprehended in depth almost immediately begins to erode whatever security was derived from the concrete, fear-based thinking. Instead, one feels, so to speak, as though—the ground having been taken from under one's feet—one has merely hastily snatched whatever weapons were handy, rushed to assume a fighting stance, only to discover the would-be weapon beginning to dissolve in one's grasp.

This secondary anxious reaction unconsciously can seem to mock the initial certainty of fear: as though to say it is what you do not know, your ignorance, and not what you know that is important here, that is dangerous and will undo you. Thus, anxiety insidiously shifts the emphasis from fear-based decisiveness to the helplessness and hopelessness of the ego (fear it could be said is manic, anxiety is melancholic). What starts out as fear--the sense that, although there is a threatening target before one, it is nevertheless within one's sights, contained in an ego-centered context that is broader than it is and has at its disposal a number of strategies with which to combat or at least attenuate its menace—begins to lose its grip on the object as it shifts to anxiety. In anxiety, the ratio between you and what you fear flip-flops: it is the context, instead, or more accurately the atmosphere that seems to dominate, while the self, by comparison, seems inconsequential and puny, as though groping in an uncanny psychic fog like the felt presence of uncertainty).

This can be summed up in the following unconscious equations. Fear = what's wrong with this picture?: find and correct the one thing in an otherwise predictable and safe world. Anxiety = everything is wrong with this picture: the very reality it depicts is alien and hostile.

I have tried to show how the dynamics of anxiety opens the person up to extraordinary vulnerability, in part because he or she feels helpless and powerless.

In itself this is not surprising inasmuch as the structural relations between the ego and its defense mechanisms to a large extent are based on brute psychic power (I have written about this elsewhere in *Power Plays*, Alper, 1998). It is therefore a short step to see how someone who is so-inclined—by capitalizing on and turning to his or her advantage—can make this universal chink in our psychic armor into a power game.

GETTING IN THE LAST WORD

Although patients tend to be especially sensitive to this, as they are to every kind of real or imagined slight, we are all familiar with the experience. Someone, for example, tries to address some instance of injustice that has been weighing on their mind, and are immediately told, "That's water under the bridge". Or someone indicates they do not understand something that has been said and are told, "I've already answered that". Or someone protests that something that was supposed to be done, that directly affects them, was not done and are informed, "That doesn't concern you".

It can easily be infuriating when someone else unexpectedly and imperiously gets in the last word. Not only does such a person act as though they are the one entitled to put whatever interaction is being transacted in perspective by offering a final summary comment, they apparently insist upon it. The impression is thereby created that there is a verbal race of sorts taking place and whoever gets to the finish line first will win. Making a point of getting in the last word thereby immediately thrusts the conversation into an adversarial mode. It highlights there can be no mutuality, compromise or working things out. There can only be a winner and, by inference, a loser.

Ironically, the maneuver—meant to convey power and authority—typically achieves the opposite effect. The other senses the person is much too aggressively self-absorbed to entertain in any fair way what is being expressed and sees the attempt to impress through the tactic of controlling who can make closure, as a transparent gambit. What, however, makes it all the more irritating is that—as a power game—it is deceptively and disarmingly effective. Because to counter pseudo closure, the other is placed in the awkward position of accomplishing at least two separate tasks almost simultaneously: challenging the assumption that anything has been resolved; and reopening and starting up an issue that is bound to draw resistance from the person.

In addition, by thereby refusing to let the person get in the last word, it can easily seem as though you yourself are being motivated by exactly the same impulse. In turn, this can engender a defensive mind set in which one tires to anticipate the future of the interaction so as to head off the expected one-up-manship. In order to make such defensiveness work, however, it becomes necessary to deny that one is being either defensive or competitive: one is merely seeking to achieve proper closure, not to get in the last word. Not surprisingly, few can pull this off. To do so one has often to struggle, lawyer-like, to create a plausible conversational facade of jury-rigged logic wherein each response—to escape the charge of being subjective—must be seemingly rational and objective.

For all of these reasons, the effectiveness of getting in the last word is that it can quickly induce the other to begin to feel like he or she really does not want to compete on this level. At which point the person who initiated the pseudo closure will often draw back and condescendingly act as though they are the one giving in to the other (thereby getting in the last word again). And at this juncture the person typically wins because: they are better than their opponent at this particular game, evidenced by the fact that the other—once sucked into it—usually gets visibly more upset and competitive.

THE POWER OF CONTEMPT

As a psychotherapist you are often presented with internalized images, scenes and scenarios that are fueled by and are primarily expressions of contempt of one person for another. A woman can no longer stand the sight of the man with whom she has been living the past six years and feels like her skin crawls the moment he enters the room. A man feels so humiliated and toyed with at his job that he spends hours each week elaborating a fantasy in which he simultaneously hands in his letter of resignation and spits in the face of his flabbergasted boss.

An unemployed graduate student, enraged at his parents who have just financially cut him off, gleefully and spitefully contemplates going on welfare just to shake up their despicable bourgeois values. A woman, deeply disappointed in a boyfriend who has steadfastly refused for years to make a commitment, concludes, and coldly announces to all of their mutual friends, that she now realizes he was probably gay. An actor, who can no longer tolerate what he considers the rejection of his peers, decides to cut off his friends and embrace the life of a recluse. And so on.

Objects of contempt such as these are not found but constructed. Like a frozen caricature of the offending party's worst flaws, they represent an inner refusal to admit or include redeeming features. The weight of the contempt is perhaps most clearly felt in its concentrated, judgmental harshness. Manifestly, the object of contempt has done something, or a series of actions, that has left an almost palpable psychical stench in the mind of the person. The contempt as such is not only a refusal to revise in any way, soften or humanize one's perspective on the history of the relationship, but more significantly it is a refusal to move forward, to consider a possible future with the other (reminiscent of Christopher Bollas' concept of the terminal object in his brilliant discussion of obsessionalism, 1995).

Contempt for the other as an internalized state of mind is usually perceived to have originated reactively: one did not have contempt a priori; one found contempt forced upon one by behavior so offensive it could not be ignored. By holding a particular object—an individual or an act—in contempt one distances oneself from it, not enough to be indifferent, but enough to be able to be safely hateful.

It is worth noting the condemned internal object cannot fight back—denuded not only of complexity, humanism, but of life itself—and stands as a kind of effigy for someone who in the flesh is always considerably more dangerous, regardless of how passive or dependent they may be upon the contemptuous person. Psychically sticking pins into an internalized, deadened object, however, invariably leaves a hollow feeling. What the person really wants—as Harry Stack Sullivan once noted (1956)—is for the other to not only know but feel the humiliation that is being projected on them, but this, of course, requires a fairly substantial investment of one's energies. Which is why, even in a frankly sadomasochistic relationship where contempt is both expressed and acted out, there is almost always a huge discrepancy between the inner experience and the honest communication of the wish to degrade the other.

Another way to say this is that there is often a secret component—lending a paranoid flavor—to one's contempt: and in order to justify the sense of paranoid secrecy one may unconsciously intensify the scorn that is felt, as though to prove that the other is not worth the investment and respect implied by open communication. One then relates more to the inner object of contempt than to the actual other. In spite of this, as a state of mind, it is not introspective; as an emotion, it has the external thrust of punitive anger. It works by sealing off and not dealing with the past. What is important is not the history and complexity of the relationship but the offenses that were committed.

It follows there is a need to compensate for one's narcissistic injuries by periodically identifying with one's inner rage. Having contempt works in the same way that being put upon or exasperated works: the desire for punitive release is so compelling that it does not allow for simultaneous reflection upon what one is doing and thinking. Any nascent impulse towards interpersonal mutuality is likely to be obliterated by dint of the principle of reciprocal inhibition. Contempt may therefore be viewed as frozen indignation. By feeling only irritation, criticism, dismissal, and a restless wish to punish the other, there can be no room for empathic interchange: such thoughts simply do not occur.

For all of these reasons, the network of associated feelings—narcissistic injury, fear, rage, humiliation and so on—that preceded the consolidation of contempt does not come into play or rather gets whited out by the impulsive and expulsive nature of the overruling, judgmental state of mind. And contempt—the more one relies upon it to contain the disturbing affects that are engendered by the other—is reinforced and increasingly sensitized. So that eventually it can react with hair-trigger responsiveness to any hint of tension or uneasiness emanating from the despised other. At the same time, it goes nowhere. Since, by its nature, it is rarely discharged, it is regularly accompanied by a gnawing frustration. One tends therefore to feel thwarted, bottled up in the contempt that is in one. One may begin to feel contempt for the contempt one has as one realizes he or she has been driven to feel the way they do. And the fact that the other is held responsible for the necessity in the first place to harbor contempt, becomes a further cause for contempt.

Relationship To One's Contempt

It is dramatic to have contempt, not unlike being the secret director of an internal, mini soap opera. Although too painful an emotion to be felt continuously, it can function in the manner of a grudge, providing—when activated—a quick and exciting burst of psychic energy. Not the least of its secondary benefits is that it is, more or less, accessible whenever one needs it. Entertaining flat out contempt is dramatic because it violates, as mentioned, one of society's abiding canons: you always give the other—especially when they have fallen into disfavor—a fair chance to redeem themselves and to redress past wrongs. By contrast, the dynamics of contempt are reminiscent of what Christopher Bollas (1993) terms the fascist state of mind: there is the endless, stimulating and cathartic flogging of an impotent internal object. (It is a relief that one can seemingly contain, process and then express the most hateful parts of one's mind just like any other emotion.)

Part of the contempt one feels is that the other apparently doesn't realize the depth of contempt in which he or she is held. Indeed, they must be clueless as to what is really going on if they continue to have anything to do with such a merciless critic. But it is a short step from this to wonder why they themselves have anything to do with such a despicable other, why they cannot be more direct concerning their true feelings and why they do not seem to be able to cleanly break off a relationship that is so consistently unsatisfying. And to the degree they are made aware they have a need to harbor contempt, they may become the target of their own judgmentalism.

Not surprisingly, a defense against this is denial: one is not being mean-spirited, one simply has strong principles and cannot help reacting passionately when they are sullied. Being capable of contempt, therefore, can be viewed as proof—analogous to the display of courage—that one can respond, when appropriate, with powerful unambiguous emotions, that one has soul, is a moralist, does not suffer fools or low-lifes lightly, has pride, can make, if necessary, an independent if secret decision concerning the true value of a relationship and, perhaps most important of all, that one is to be feared. (No small part of the pleasure of having contempt is the accompanying fantasy of just how shocked the other would be if they could know the extent of the disdain in which they are held.)

Someone who acts out their contempt typically does so in a matter-of-fact manner, as though they are expressing something so manifestly obvious that it is close to public knowledge. And once again the refusal to be subtle once one does show contempt, the seeming disdain for the other's capacity to retaliate, make it a formidable power game.

THE DENIAL OF A RELATIONSHIP

One of the most effective ways to control a relationship is to deny that one exists, and a common strategy for achieving this is to act as though whatever is going on interactively is devoid of any real meaning or intimacy. Thus, in a classic illustration of this tactic, someone who is leery of getting involved and wants to make sure the other knows this is only a business transaction, asks "What can I do for you?" In one fell swoop, the person sends the message: there will be no mutuality here; at most, they will respond to, react or reflect upon what the other introduces. Such a person strengthens their pose of detachment by behaving as though they are primarily interested in relating to, facilitating or clarifying what the other is doing. When appropriate, they may express a puzzlement or actively question what they profess not to understand.

In this manner, the person denies that there is reciprocal communication between them. The implication is that it is the other—and not the couple—who is in need and who is seeking gratification. And the implied reproach is that the person is being narcissistically employed as a means to a selfish end. By asserting a presumed lack of parity vis-á-vis need satisfaction, he or she justifies the refusal to simply collaborate or comply with whatever is being sought. To in effect suggest that someone is being predominantly motivated by self-interest is therefore to deny that a meaningful interpersonal link exists. In turn, the other is left to either further articulate or defend their behavior, thus taking the spotlight off the covert attempt to denigrate the potential value of the interaction.

In short, such invalidation is unconsciously intended as prima facie evidence that there is not a relationship, and the other—who typically does not want to be objectified in this manner—is placed in the untenable position of trying to be the advocate of meaning and intentionality for two people.

"I'M BORED"

In his famous book of psychiatric, poetic despair (Knots, 1970), R.D. Laing comments on the person who feigns boredom as an interpersonal ploy for gaining attention: "In trying to be interesting, you are *very* boring. You are frightened of being boring, you try to be interesting by not being interested, but are interested only in not being boring."

From the standpoint of our theme, there is power to be had by simply affecting disinterest in what matters to people. Thus, someone, asked whether they have seen a current hit movie, laconically answers, "I couldn't sit through it. I walked out." Or at the merest mention of an international celebrity's name, volunteers the opinion, "I can't stand her." Or, upon hearing of the publication of the latest legal thriller, announces, "I try to stay away from junk literature."

To be bored is to assume a superordinate position over the other person who has been innocently taken in. Denying that personal, relational, or intimacy issues are at stake, the bored individual suggests instead that he or she is a kind of consumer of experience, a voyeur in search of adequate stimulation. Deficiency as such is thereby neatly externalized: the deficit is without, the failure is of the object to engage and not of the spectator who cannot be motivated to invest in a meaningful way.

By contrast, a way to understand the defensive uses of the state of being bored is to look at all the things one, by implication, cannot be so long as one is making a point of being disinterested: one is not insecure, vulnerable, anxious, herself boring, depressed, in need of sorting out or confronting uncomfortable feelings. Indeed, someone who is bored may at various times feel: intelligent in the sense that they are discriminating; autonomous inasmuch as they are exercising choice; tough-minded in that they are not afraid to call a spade a spade; communicative in that they can sum up their experience in a simple, evocative way leaving no doubt as to what is meant; provocative in that people often do not want to hear and are not expecting such a dismissive response; authoritative in that it is hard to imagine anyone changing their mind, or being persuaded to do so, after such a declaration; able to cut to the chase where another might flounder; and, finally, as showing they do not lack confidence when it comes to being critical.

For all of these reasons, to profess boredom is to be a conversational killer—the underlying message being that everything that has to be said has just been said and there is therefore nothing further to talk about. Even more to the point, that there is no interest in whatever the other may think about the matter. It follows, from an interpersonal standpoint, the statement is blatantly narcissistic: the pronouncement of someone's ennui, intended to be noted and perhaps admired but certainly not related to. Furthermore, there may be a seed of doubt planted in the other's mind that sometimes they are perceived as boring.

To be publicly bored, therefore, is to be off-putting, if not intimidating. More often than not it immediately terminates whatever interpersonal momentum had been achieved just prior to its appearance. By introducing a detached, critical and decidedly unempathic frame of mind, it drives the other a little backwards. There is an unavoidable coldness to the bored state of mind, requiring one, as it does, to be completely irresponsive to whatever may be appealing, human, vulnerable, emotional or evocative about whatever is being appraised. But since there is almost always some redeeming feature to any expressive sample of human life—which, by definition, is a complex ensemble of many elements—this entails at least temporarily, or selectively, shutting off any empathic receptivity to every aspect of the object that is being evaluated. What this means, it should be obvious, is that to affect boredom is to adopt an attitude that is the antithesis of someone who is empathic and nurturing. Under the cover that one has an autonomous right to voice one's opinion, whether pro or con, an implicit threat is delivered that one does not suffer fools lightly and this generally carries far more weight in the recipient's unconscious than the supposed informational merit of the critical assessment.

When one moves, however, from the aesthetic to the interpersonal, there may be no more potent power game than to introduce one's state of boredom as a barometer of an ongoing, serious relationship. An unconscious toxic equation is thus brought into play: boredom = no longer stimulated = no longer in love or having respect. To profess boredom in the other is to elevate stimulus craving and entertainment value above interrelating. This is an insidious change of definition undercutting some of the key ingredients of the presumed intimacy—commitment, attunement, containment of immediate frustration so as to focus on the process and long term benefits of the interaction (the opposite dynamics, it should be noted, of someone who is unashamedly seeking greater stimulation)—that often goes unnoticed because it creates such an instant narcissistic wound in the other. Even worse than indifference, a show of boredom can be analogous to witnessing someone being actively turned off (like holding one's psychical nose in your presence).

Using Boredom As A Ploy

The dynamics:

There is simultaneously a denial of responsibility to the other and the unconscious activation of selfish interests. The person begins to think of herself as primarily a receptacle, aware of a stimulus deprivation that requires immediate external, narcissistic supplies. At the same time, the person does not feel an obligation to reciprocate with similar narcissistic supplies. The stimulus deprivation of the other is a non-issue because—so long as he or she is being placed in the role of a performer—there can be room for only one spectator.

Examples:

1. "My feelings for you have changed."

Although the person does not outright say she is suffering from boredom—which may be considered needlessly insulting—this comes to the same thing: in one fell swoop all the ingredients of intimacy are waived aside and simple, dumb feelings have become the only referent that matters. The implication being that these feelings are too unsophisticated, raw and honest to lie and she therefore has no other choice but to follow their hints. And for the other to ask her to change her decision to leave the relationship, in effect would be tantamount to asking her to be false to her heart.

2. "Nothing is forever."

Here the person deftly externalizes and sacrifices individual responsibility and commitment to an impersonal, so-called law of life: the only constant is change. The message is that variety—if not the spice—is the inevitable byproduct of life. Analogously, it is suggested that transience and flux are the stuff of relating. Relationships, therefore, if they are to fit in with the ebb and flow, the cyclical dynamics of love, must be modified, transformed and when appropriate, relinquished. Commitment is thereby subtly equated with structural rigidity, resistance to growth and psychic deadness. Terminating a moribund relationship is presented as healthy change. The decision not to see someone anymore is to be considered merely the exercising of a viable option. Love objects, according to such a manifestly self-serving philosophy, become means to an end, servants to a process of exploration, growth, stasis, change and rebirth. What is paramount is the process and the satisfaction that it delivers or doesn't deliver. And people are either way stations or impediments along the road to gratification and pleasure.

3. "My needs are not being met."

Here the person does not say they are bored, but starved. The deprivation is one of basic psychological nutriments, not of gratuitous stimulation. It is hoped that this may be less offensive—inasmuch as needs by definition are something that have to be met—whereas the desire not to be bored is seen as something less central to the well being of the self.

What these examples have in common is that they exploit, in one fashion or another, the power of affecting boredom to seriously tarnish an existing relationship.

BEING CONDESCENDING

Everyone, at certain times, to a greater or lesser extent, has experienced the pain and humiliation of being treated in a demeaning fashion. Understandably, they are then immediately thrown on the defensive. To be condescending, therefore, is not only to radically withdraw any possible narcissistic supplies, but to confront the other with a toxic lack of nurturance and empathy; the implicit message being it is obvious the other does not merit any positive consideration. It is a variation of having contempt, but it differs inasmuch as it is often unconsciously expressed and—when confronted—is almost always vigorously denied.

By hiding what would otherwise be a glaring deficit when it comes to being nurturing, the condescending person strategically turns the tables: it is the other who is eliciting and even inviting the display of contempt. Hence, someone who condescends acts as though he is merely reacting to something putrid in the self of another. He does not admit he has a need to feel contempt, to projectively identify with contempt in others, to fend off contempt he feels for parts of himself and so on.

Being condescending works as a power game because it engenders in the other a dread that they are about to have an unbearably negative identity forced upon them. Furthermore, it is intimidating that such a person can seemingly be so sure of himself: having arrived at an opinion that is not only independent of but radically at odds with what its subject—who, after all, is the only real expert—actually thinks. As though this judgmental person has access to some higher source of knowledge that transcends what can be legitimately learned from the interpersonal field.

Needless to say, it is demoralizing to realize that nothing one might say or do could modify the condescending view that has been arrived at. The essential authority of the other—the potential impact deriving from the freedom to express and elaborate the true self—is thereby radically undercut. In effect, this is to be rendered *psychically redundant* (reminiscent of Christopher Bollas' concept of the "useless mind", 1993). To be condescending is therefore to evoke the unreachable, punitive superego, lashing out in frozen contempt at what it takes for the anti-ego ideal. Not surprisingly, it is a hallmark of the self-imposed authority of the condescending person that he or she manifests no wish to consult with the object of their scorn. It is as though the condescension is its own court of last appeal, as though the sheer force of the contempt displayed and felt is proof that something real (and rotten) must have prompted it (where there's smoke, there's fire).

Looked at this way, the other whom one encounters and who is inexplicably judgmental, cannot help but echo some of the deepest, most painful and deprived memories of our internal relations with our own harsh superego: its strictly unilateral way of dealing with us; its indifference to and inability to empathize with our pain; the lack of ambivalence, aura of certainty and unwavering nature of its views; the fact that whatever it knows it seems to know beforehand (in an eerie way, therefore, the knowledge it has seems a priori and cannot be contradicted by new experience). A good question to ask, therefore, is are we in any way recognized as individuals by our punitive superegos or are we simply dealt with as impersonal offenders of some jealously guarded principles? Are we dealt with as violators of rules or as selves? Do our superegos relate to us or to this set of higher rules? Do our superegos punish us, as they are supposed to, "for our own good", in the service of making us better people, or are they just narcissistically protecting and preserving an arbitrary, but fixed code of conduct?

Because one naturally tends to become defensively self-absorbed when caught up in relations with one's superego, one usually does not pay attention to it as a separate psychical agency. It goes unnoticed, therefore, that our superegos tend to be faceless, unidimensional, lacking in dramatic presence, and without any of the saving graces—sense of humor, warmth, spontaneity—that denote the simply human. And, not surprisingly, most people would be hard put to describe the characteristics of their superego, especially, how it might compare with that of other people. That is, they do not as a rule differentiate and are not so much interested in their superego in its own right, as they are in its effect upon themselves and others.

It follows they are in the dark as to its underlying nature. Does it, for example, possess emotion? If so, it would appear to be anger. Is there any other way to relate to it rather than as a sacred rule which must not be violated? Is it to be understood as essentially just a disembodied principle, with a life of its own, that somehow has been inculcated into their mind? It is worth noting that people do not think in terms of narcissistically wounding one's superego, but of enraging it. They do not think of talking to, engaging or spending time with their superego. And they apparently accept that their superego is mute as readily as they accept that God is mute. But, after all, one appeals and sometimes prays to God ... maintains a fantasy that He may be hovering around and earnestly listening in a way one does not with one's conscience.

For all of these reasons, we do not tend to think of what is supposedly the highest part of our psyche as itself being human: ironically, one of the worst things we could say about another is that he or she is acting in such a way as to remind us of our own conscience: they are forever being judgmental. Another way to say this is that someone who represented for us just this singular aspect—the voice of conscience—would strike us as most likely monstrous.

But then, one may unconsciously wonder, isn't this voice in my head, my voice? Aren't I the very self that it speaks for? Yes, we may answer, but if so, why does it speak in such a detached and disembodied way? If it does represent the self, why not all the self—the warm, human, vulnerable and lovable parts—as well as the less deserving ones? Why is it such a Johnny-one-note, monomaniacal voice? And the answer suggests itself that—masked by the judgmental force of the superego—lies a structural impoverishment.

Interestingly enough, this is reflected in the apparent paucity of the professional literature when it comes to the developmental, especially nurturing and empathic elements of the superego (one notable exception is Christopher Bolas; see his brilliant essay, "The Self As Object", 1987). While we talk of the precursor, the pathology, the primitiveness of the superego, we say comparatively little about its fate once it has been established (compare this to the almost inexhaustible attention that is paid to the vicissitudes of cognitive and ego development).

In other words, as professionals, we seem to keep our distance—in theory as well as in our inner lives—from our superegos. But we tend to reciprocate, it leaks out in spite of ourselves that we don't really like our superegos: we write coolly, with reserve and rarely—except perhaps for the papers of Freud or when we are busy depicting the sadomasochism of our relations to our own superegos or our patients to theirs—does the concept come alive. That is, we are critical of it as it is of us, but our criticism shows itself as indifference or psychic deadness. (This, of course, is a general statement and does not include all those who are moralistic or to whom—being unbending, punitive, judgmental or sadomasochistic—is ego syntonic).

It follows what the person who is condescending does is to borrow some of this terrible psychical power and—by personifying it—to turn it into a potent weapon. And it is interesting that the other does not challenge the act of condescension per se, so much as the party's right to exercise it: thus, "Who do you think you are to treat me this way?" It is worth noting the other does not say that no one has the right to be so condescending, only that this person has not earned the right. Because everyone has experienced parental rejection and indifference—internalized and memorialized in the frozen inaccessibility of the aloof, implacable and forever judging superego—there is an unconscious dread and readiness to accept, and a disinclination to contest or examine the meaning of the condescension one encounters (analogous to how we do not challenge the right of our conscience to exercise its judgment). There may be no better way, therefore, for putting the other on the defensive, while hiding ourselves, than to be condescending.

CHAPTER TWO

Who Wins, Who Loses

DYNAMICS OF POWER GAMES

Here let me briefly summarize what I went into exhaustively in my book, *Power Plays:*

They tend to be over quickly. Of necessity, they are characterized by impatience—like narcissistic giving—as an unconscious strategy to protect an underlying fragility from being exposed. There is cynicism regarding the possibility of being autonomously nurtured, in turn giving rise to a need to coerce compliance (what I have called behavioral puppetry). A glaring lack of respect, often open contempt for the uses of empathy. Indeed, interrelating is to be replaced by a kind of strategic reconnaissance of the other's buttons to be pushed, weak points to be exploited, defenses that can be attacked. To play a power game is therefore to relate to the defenses of the self, rather than to the self, with intimacy needs being considered as either annoyingly irrelevant or as an invitation and opportunity for seduction. Time itself is then regarded instrumentally and competitively, in the athlete's sense of racing against the clock (in distinct contrast to the occasion for intimacy wherein time is unconsciously viewed as an evocative field in which closeness may be facilitated: time as incubation and not as a yardstick with which to measure performance).

Someone, therefore, who initiates a power game, typically may at various times feel that he or she is: courageous, not afraid to gambol and compete in a winner-take-all game; manifesting pride inasmuch as they are ready to defend what is theirs or take what they are entitled to take; tough-minded, calling a spade a spade and recognizing when force must be used; street-smart and worldly, able to spot a power play as it develops and react accordingly; realistic in the sense of perceiving that people are essentially self-centered and sophisticated in that they can see through defenses based on a pose of pseudo-altruism; caught up in a soap opera-like suspense of whether one will win or lose as one approaches their moment of truth and, finally, telling it like it is (reinforced in our culture, of course, and celebrated as healthy narcissism).

WORSHIPING THE POWER GOD WITHIN

One thinks of one's inner power as a source of surplus energy or psychic force. An ace up the sleeve. A bodyguard. Something that can be brought to bear in case someone needs to be taught a lesson. Typically the power one has is manifested as an effect on the self: recognized externally by its impact on others and internally by a sense of feel-good mastery.

Power does not tend to be thought of as an element of one's identity, a feature of one's character, but rather as a reward one receives for the acquisition of certain indispensable life skills. It is sometimes thought of as a weapon one has access to that should only be used in special circumstances. The exercise of one's power therefore requires justification in the sense that the exercise of one's intelligence does not. When it does come into play, more often than not, its purpose is to change the interpersonal status quo of the context in which it arises. From this perspective, it is an accelerator of whatever process someone is involved in (including, of course, the reactions of others).

The influence of one's power is viewed pragmatically and functionally. If its effects are not visible; if there are no known consequences, it does not exist. While someone may have worked hard over a period of years in order to achieve it—once they have it—they are supposed to be able to harness it quickly. Unconsciously personal power can be equated with a button that one pushes: not something you invest in or cultivate, but simply unsheathe.

For all of these reasons, power is often regarded as a psychic force, waiting to be channeled. It is an offer that cannot be refused for someone who finds himself or herself placed in a position of authority, who has been assigned a difficult role to execute or is required to perform at a stressful level. When the exercise of one's power, however, is not so specifically defined—as, for example, in the welter of everyday interpersonal relations—the issue is scarier and people are unsure of how and when to rely upon it. Accordingly, they tend to avoid taking responsibility for its use by pointing whenever they can to some external circumstance or necessity of life. They are most comfortable when they are seemingly being carried along and riding on its crest.

Since one's personal power is often thought of as an unconscious force, there an be a temptation to use its mindlessly or with as little foresight as possible. As a result, the vicissitudes of power are usually rooted in the here and now and are often a short-sighted affair. Its goal—like political office—seems not to extend further than keeping itself intact (and in office especially when challenged). And it aims, whenever it can, for immediate discharge.

STRATEGIES FOR WINNING

What follows are examples showing some common unconscious strategies for acquiring or sustaining interpersonal power.

DROPPING THE INFORMATION BOMB

This occurs when someone—a lover, a boss, a doctor—breaks the worst possible news to you (e.g., "I no longer want to see you" ... "I'm letting you go" ... "The tumor is malignant") in the shortest amount of time, without any apparent interest in discussing it farther. Since the information cannot possibly be assimilated in the allotted time, it arrives with an explosive effect. Or rather, the information per se can be almost instantaneously understood on an intellectual level, but the staggering repercussions so far as one's emotions are concerned cannot begin to be processed.

As a result the auditor is immediately put into a double bind: on the one hand her pressing need for information in the first place has just been met in the most unequivocal fashion possible, thereby making any request for further clarifications seem redundant and perhaps demanding; on the other hand, the even greater need to adjust to and absorb the shock waves of the information bomb that has just been dropped—which cannot be done without some minimal empathic collaboration on the part of the one who made the decision to radically break the worst possible news—is deliberately, if subtly refused: the person withholds additional information under the cover that there seems to be little else to say.

It is obvious that the bearer of a heartbreaking message is looking to escape from the obligation to relate: that is, to soften the blow, to put what can easily be taken as a monumental personal rejection in perspective (e.g., by mentioning all the legitimate positives that were there, by carefully pointing out the impersonal factors—ones having nothing to do with the particular individual or her assets—but which were decisive when it came to making the decision to reject and so on).

By contrast, an empathic refusal would recognize that the recipient needs some real recovery time for the considerable narcissistic injury that has just been sustained and would endeavor to facilitate such a recovery by making it clear that the person was available for whatever help could be afforded. Part of an empathic refusal, of course, is the acknowledgment that the person is responsible—to the extent that presumably he made an autonomous choice to drop the information bomb, when he could have gone the other way—for the narcissistic injury delivered.

This is one reason why what we are calling an empathic refusal, especially when it is generally not required, as is the case in the business and professional world, is so rarely encountered: because it entails the integration of two almost antithetical elements—impersonal rejection and empathy. To avoid the substantial psychic work that this requires, the person, typically, opts for power (which is always a handy interpersonal shortcut). That is, as though his participation in the final decision was an entirely objective affair, one that does not entail a need for relating, he denies he is responsible for any narcissistic injury incurred by the other (which, it is implied is a purely private reaction). In short, under the pretext of communicating something that needs to be said, the person drops the information bomb, withdraws and attempts to wipe his hands of the matter as quickly as possible.

The common denominator in all these cases is that they are variants in one way or another of what might be called damning Noes, moreover, Noes that are almost completely torn out of any conceivable empathic interpersonal context that might cushion the blow. That they are nakedly dropped is hardly coincidental: it allows the messenger of terrible news, under the cover of a power umbrella, to mask the fact that he or she is incapable of relating and showing empathy when perhaps it is most needed. A very fundamental reason, however, that people usually avoid even trying to be empathic on such traumatic occasions is simply that it is painful to do so. Once someone begins to feel any realistic empathy for the narcissistic injury that is being unavoidably engendered in the other, they simultaneously realize the intimidating discrepancy between the huge disappointment that is being experienced and the scant help—even if they wanted to give it—that can be offered.

This may be best seen in the characteristically inept way doctors traditionally deliver the worst possible medical news: when the discontinuity, say, between the fact that a patient is going to or likely to die soon and the comfort that he or she can now offer (having just said that) is of tragic proportions. And compounding this is the awareness that the doctor and whatever solace he or she can presently offer is perhaps the only and last hope the panic-stricken patient has. If the doctor announces what seems at first blush to be a death sentence and then withdraws into a benign resignation, the patient receives the message that the final person who might offer hope, has no hope to offer.

So, what might be an empathic response instead? First of all, to recognize that regardless of how inadequate a doctor's empathy may be to the crisis at hand, at perhaps no other time, as mentioned, is it more valued. An empathic response would take into account that the patient is likely to be traumatized by the tragic news—and therefore susceptible to distorted, persecutory fantasies as to what lies in store—so that any realistic prognosis, noting hopeful, howsoever slight, as well as dire possibilities, would have to be at least minimally reassuring.

Thus: "From thirty to sixty percent of people with your condition can go on, with proper treatment, to live between ten to fifteen years. Twenty percent are completely curable and never have a recurrence. However, the detection has been early in your case, so that increases your chances of recovery. Now here's what you have to do."

Doctors, of course, rarely do that because what we have been describing is a matter of relating, not prescribing or treating.

All of which can be summed up by saying that when something that is essentially interpersonal is arbitrarily framed as a medium for the exchange of information, the message is that interrelating is irrelevant.

PROVIDING USELESS INFORMATION

This is perhaps the other side of the coin of dropping the information bomb. Although, when applicable, few things can be as meaningful as negative information—the most famous example coming from the doctor who reports, "The tumor is benign"—when gratuitous, few things can be as useless. Useless information is especially toxic when it is presented as though it is a direct response to a question that has been urgently asked. It most commonly occurs within a business or professional setting wherein one is deemed to hold the answer to a very important question but, for any of a variety of reasons, does not show the slightest inclination to divulge it. Thus, an aspiring job applicant who has been attempting for months to find out if there is any interest in hiring him is told by the secretary of the man who originally interviewed him, "I gave him your message." Or an author who has been waiting for half a year for a response to his manuscript—and who at last is put in contact with the editor who's supposed to have read it—is informed, "It's sitting here in a pile on my desk." Or an actor who calls a casting director to find out why he was finally turned down, after a number of call backs, for an important part and is told, "I never give critiques on the telephone."

In all such cases, the underlying dynamics are similar: The first stage is deception. The person invariably acts as though the information that is being provided is not only germane, but is exactly what is being asked for: in other words, the entire responsibility for the value or lack of value of what is being communicated is shifted onto the other. The usefulness of the information, therefore, according to the person is not in question (and this, of course, makes it extremely difficult for the other to challenge: for if the information really is beside the point, why did they waste both their time by asking for it in the first place)?

In the second stage, the person—after having dispensed useless information—presumes that closure has been reached, typically, by matter-of-factly changing the subject. Should the other choose to resist such pseudo closure by raising further questions, a familiar ploy is to not only reiterate what has just been said but to provide additional but equally useless information: e.g., (in the case of the casting director), "The reason I don't give actors critiques of their auditions is that I don't find it helpful."

From the point of view of one who is thus left in the dark, the unconscious message can be: "I have nothing to say to you" ... or "Ask a stupid question and you'll get a stupid answer". The receiving of useless information, especially when one is in need of a thoughtful, considerate and candid reply, can easily seem a travesty of the act of giving, a covert attempt to trivialize the gravity of the other's need. In spite of which, someone can never be sure whether the information is as useless as it sounds or whether he simply doesn't yet know enough to appreciate its value. Compounding the dilemma is that such negative information is frequently relayed in the most authoritative manner possible, making it that much more difficult to contest.

It is worth noting at this point that the dispersal of information—useful or not—has some characteristic, often unconscious interpersonal effects:

Foremost, as mentioned, is that it signals that issues of intimacy and interrelating are to be at least temporarily suspended. This is accomplished by the almost instantaneous shifting of the perspective to a purely cognitive domain. To be then primarily informational means: to switch off any access to the affective unconscious (to what Christopher Bollas has called unconscious freedom). And it does this by presenting or evoking a compelling, puzzle-solving, alternative world that is never far from consciousness, that obviously has a lot to do with our survival in general and success in any particular pursuit. (See Daniel Dennett, in particular, *Kinds of Minds*, 1996, for a marvelous survey and tour of some of the cognitive wonders that underwrite ordinary everyday life.)

It may therefore be, as Dennett says, that the cognitive mode of receiving the world is so basic to our survival and has been so evolutionarily embedded in us that once it is clearly activated—as may be the case when, presumably, even trivial information is being disseminated—it can naturally drown out any competing, non-cognitive, especially emotive, unconscious, interpersonal system. And while the unconscious, of course, never sleeps and is at work during cognitive operations, it does tend to get tuned out: *that is, information rejects the participation of the unconscious.*

What Bollas once brilliantly said about the dynamics of an obsession—one idea follows another, but they do not follow unconsciously—can also be said about every basic cognitive function and every bit of information. One idea follows another, one concept fits into another, one fact gives rise to a second but almost always consciously and predictably. For all of these reasons, information tends to seem, especially in comparison to the imprecise psyche and even murkier unconscious, to be attractively hard-edged and clean. Information, therefore (as a kind of always accessible parallel universe) promises a ready escape from the blurrings and uncertainties of the subjective psyche. And sometimes (to paraphrase Fairbairn, 1943)—"It is better to be a sinner in a world ruled by God, than to live in a world ruled by the Devil"—a person would rather be wrong (by, for example, receiving useless information) in a straightforward, common sense world than right in a world that has no unchanging and unambiguous reference points (e.g., the psychical world).

To this extent, information, even if useless, is seductive. It offers the possibility for immediate gratification: if it is useful, you can know it right away and if not, one has obtained negative information which at least may have potential application. (This is because the amount of available information is exponentially beyond the assimilative powers of any one individual. Which in turn means that even in the best case scenario only an infinitesimal fraction of all available, recorded knowledge will be accessible to any single person. However, in order to get to that usable fraction, it will be necessary to somehow not get bogged down in all the rest. While it is always hoped one can—vis-á-vis a well-timed and well-aimed question—cut a straight path to the desired answer, in reality one will have to accept that often one will never reach the optimal information. From such a pessimistic but practical standpoint, negative information can be a quite helpful, winnowing process: if it is efficient, if it serves to condense many irrelevant facts into a single category that can then be bypassed, it can indirectly steer the person to what is important.)

Hence, the contemporary reluctance to overlook any fact that may somehow, unsuspectedly, lead to another fact that will eventually point the way to something productive and life-enhancing and it is this which makes the giving of useless information an almost irresistibly easy power game for anyone who is thought to be in possession of a specialized knowledge of any kind.

MUTING THE OTHER

Recently, a highly agitated, thirty-five year old man who considered himself to be at a crossroads came to see me for a consultation. In the session, he spoke at a feverish pace, punctuating what seemed to be an unending series of dramatic effects with sweeping, florid gestures. Born and raised in a poor Italian village, he had come to America seven years ago in order to make his fortune. Through force of will he had overcome his poverty and secured a rounded education. He considered himself secretly brilliant. In New York, he became the manager of a highly successful restaurant and was known for his charm, his ebullience and, especially, for his "people skills".

But his ambition was as boundless as it was unspecific. He wanted to return to Italy a wealthy man. To buy a home, some land, to found a community. His philanthropic dream was to teach poor, illiterate peasants the life skills, the wisdom he had acquired for himself and so pass it on. But the clock was running. In a year his green card would expire. If he did not find a woman who would agree to marry him by that time, he would be forced to return to Italy without the fortune he needed to launch his dreams. But it could not, however, be just any woman. Even though it would be in part what is called a green card marriage, he would not settle for someone who did not share his passion, what he referred to as his philosophy of life and who did not recognize his burning need to achieve great things.

In any life story, especially one such as this, there cannot help but be things that don't add up, manifest self-contradictions, and confusion. Not only from the perspective of the uninitiated listener, but also from the narrator. At such points, when it appeared obvious to both of us, that he had talked himself into a kind of corner where he was simply not making sense, he would suddenly stop, reproach himself with a rueful shake of the head and, with a mischievous grin, protest, "What can I say, Jerry? I'm Italian!"

And at first, as I think I was clearly meant to be, I was charmed, taking this for an endearing, but certainly not serious rationalization that in time, facilitated by the therapeutic process, would be supplanted by something less frivolous. But it was not to be. In subsequent sessions my patient grew not less but more preposterously exclamatory, hysterically verbose and grandiosely unrealistic. If I tried to rein in his manic flights of emotion by gently calling his attention to the multiplying lacunae between one sentence and another, between one thought and another, he would simply reiterate—as though this were by now some explanatory principle that had been established in therapy—"I'm Italian!"

I mention this patient because he conveyed to me, almost more than any other I had encountered, how it feels to be swept up in the vortex of another's emotional storms. For no matter what I could say or do, I could not seem—once he had set his affective juggernaut in motion—to make the slightest impression on him. It therefore dawned on me, from the standpoint of the theme of this book, that merely by being more emotional than the other, one can engage in a simple, though lively, power game.

The most obvious way to be more emotional is by being, as my patient was, a highly volatile personality. By flooding the other with emotion, by constantly being dramatic, someone can—if not exhaust—at least capture their attention. Just to keep up with such a tumultuous outpouring, the listener will have to process emotions that are often out of context, overreactive, self-contradictory and, perhaps most frustrating of all, self-referential.

Paradoxically, another way to be affectively dominant is by being first seemingly understated, and then unexpectedly and obliquely emotional. An example is the relatively obscure publisher of a small press who tries to introduce himself to the manager of a well-known bookstore who—after listening politely and acting as though he might be receptive to a trial sale—says, "Of course, I don't know who you are." This mix of the apparently instructional mode and hidden emotion (in this instance, quiet condescension) can be quite emasculating, typically catching the person completely off guard. How does one respond? If, for example, the choice is to answer one put-down with another—"I understand, but then I haven't heard much about you either"—the person is likely to retreat behind an icy business disclaimer, "Look, I don't have time for this. If you want to send me some promotional material you can send it to me. Otherwise, goodbye." That is, the manager, under the guise of reacting to the non-professional behavior of the small press publisher, actually raises the emotional ante by frankly rejecting the other while simultaneously pretending to be merely enacting the role of the blunt-speaking, tough-minded professional with no time to spare. This, of course, is, as it is intended to be, both infuriating and exceedingly hard to counter, leaving the other with only two bad choices: to confront the implicit condescension which would likely either instigate a fight or create a distinct animosity, thereby forfeiting, in this case, whatever chance there was for an advantageous business contact; or to pretend to accept the remark as appropriate, in effect tacitly tolerating the right of the person to be covertly abusive in the faint hope of salvaging a future benefit.

In short, flooding the other with an affect storm or slyly undercutting them with understated, disavowed put-downs are both ways of muting the other via the tactic of seizing emotional control.

THE DYNAMICS

Someone seizes control in this way by unconsciously presuming to place their finger on the emotional pulse, to sum up what is being enacted and communicated in a reductionistic manner that is meant to be both captivating and colorful: e.g., "I'm Italian!" The corollary, however, is that such a person rarely seems to find any corresponding emotional significance in what the other says or does. It follows that occupying center stage in this way not only entails being the more emotively dominating, it also means muting the emotional claims of the other: e.g., "Of course, I don't know who you are."

From the point of view of the other, there is something enormously deflating and infantilizing about having the presentation of one's emotions snuffed out like that. One may then be susceptible to a paranoid suspicion that in order for the person to really know how flimsy were the emotions being expressed, they must either be able to see into the secret self or the aspect of self being exhibited must be so meager as to be transparent to even an indifferent spectator.

The dynamics of muting the other are thus: a primary narcissistic interest in the release and satisfaction of one's own emotions accompanied by a devaluation of the worth or relevance of the other's state of mind: by not hearing, ignoring, contradicting, ridiculing, dismissing, punishing, prematurely terminating, censoring, and so forth. And when the other's emotions are paid attention to, it is typically in regard to the extent to which they resonate with and validate the person's point of view and almost never in the interest one takes in the private self of the other.

Unconsciously, therefore, the message is delivered that what is being transmitted is far more important that what is being received and that only an audience-spectator relationship is appropriate. Short of someone coming out and dramatically announcing, "I have something to say"—the classic attention-getter—this can ordinarily be accomplished in a host of unobtrusive, socially acceptable ways, all of which boil down to learning what might be called the art of writing emotional headlines: to broadcast rather than express emotions (the most common example perhaps being the well-known extrovert).

The dynamics of emotionally trumping the other are: to respond to or initiate something that manages to take the preceding interpersonal mood to a new level. By deliberately upsetting the prevailing emotional homeostasis the other is taken off guard (making it that much more difficult to adequately reply and therefore easier to top).

Examples:

1. Stonewalling. It is as effective interpersonally as it is politically to delay one's response. To make the other wait is to also weaken the relevance and

strength of the reply when it comes. It is to attempt to ensure that what you eventually say and do will occupy center stage and that you will not have to deal with any likely substantive reply. Furthermore, your actions may gain in dramatic impact by arriving serendipitously (just when the other is giving up on a response, he or she gets one).

    2. Tangential nurturing. This is something I once referred to as giving the wrong gift. The person provides undeniable gratification, but it is decidedly not what the other has asked for and needs. The intention, therefore, is to provide a substitute gratification which can compensate the other enough to deflect their attention away from the inherent frustration in not being heard. There is then always residual dissatisfaction because even if the compensatory bribe has been truly satisfying on some level, there is an unavoidable, underlying and nagging sense that one does not matter since one has not been fundamentally listened to: i.e., the so-called gift does not realistically reflect a recognition of the would-be beneficiary's need, but instead is bestowed as though it is a measure of the giver's generosity.

    3. Critiquing the other's emotive script. By unconsciously modulating the amount of visible non-verbal affirmation (relational applause) that is being registered in one another's presence, people can in effect serve as critics for each and every emotion that is being expressed. And they can do this in a manner not too different from, say, the reaction of an audience to a movie that is failing to hold their interest. That is, they begin to disconnect incrementally from what they are experiencing or they react at a pointedly less enthusiastic level than they realize the other would want them to. It follows the other will receive the impression that what they are expressing is not going over as well as they hoped and this can only have a deflating effect (even if it is unconsciously countered, as it sometimes if, by a renewed, manic attempt to overcome the person's perceived indifference).

    There are some common signs that someone is critiquing the other's emotions: by emphasizing and responding to the wrong content; by distorting or dismissing the emotive message; by being distracted, showing scant motivation to engage with what is being communicated, by appearing slightly or manifestly bored, deadened, and perhaps most important, by acting unmoved by the other's expressiveness, as though it does not resonate with and speak to one (in this regard, see Adam Phillips' wonderful observation in his *The Beast in the Nursery*, 1998, that when something speaks to you, "it makes you speak").

The antithesis of being critically detached is to become animated by how someone is expressing himself. This can perhaps be best illustrated in the case of a great artist—for example, Dylan Thomas in his *Portrait of the Artist as a Young Dog* (1984, which I have just reread)—who so overwhelms his readers with such a magical orchestration of emotional cues that they not only get it, they become lost in it (which is apropos of Wittgenstein's remark, 1980, that the genius is someone who imposes his vision on others).

Now since one of the subtexts of any interpersonal transaction, even an informational one, will involve the emotions, to the extent that there is an expressive aim there will be an effort, usually in a vague, unconscious way, to orchestrate a discrete emotional effect. That is, each person will not only endeavor to frame whatever he or she is saying or doing with a congruent tone or mood—e.g., I am now being serious, or humorous, or angry, or interesting and so on—but seek to elicit a confirmatory response from the other. And this will be so even if the intended tone is to be one of utterly objective, fact-oriented and no-nonsense professionalism (in which case the sought-after response might be that of appropriate deference combined with rapt attention). This is shown by the fact that there can be no exchange of information that is not interpersonally accompanied by a certain tone, body language and gesture which characteristically will have more to do with emotion and relationship: to convey whether one is being dominant or submissive, aggressive or deferent, friendly or indifferent, affectionate or hostile, sexually interested or not and so on vis-á-vis the other.

It now becomes immediately apparent that this spectator-other—by being able to all too easily spoil the person's mood primarily by not reflecting it—has at his or her disposal an almost universal power game.

DEADPAN

This is a variation of muting the other—the psychic equivalent of the biological analogue wherein animals play dead—although here the death that is feigned is only of the emotions. To play deadpan, of course, one must first deny that one is playing a game. (Whenever someone seriously plays a game, as Eric Berne has noted, everything is negotiable except their right to play the game.)

The potential impact, together with the dynamics of this strategy, are well illustrated in what is called deadpan humor. As every comedian knows, timing here is of the essence: knowing when the moment arrives of maximum disjunction between something that is portentous, even stunning, that cannot help but elicit a reaction and the wiped out, unbelievably neutral response known as deadpan. What then is funny is the kind of mesmerized stupidity, the monumental deflation that takes hold of the person who typically beings to act as though punched in the solar plexus by the experience. Adding to this effect is that the deadpan reaction is usually prolonged: the person is comically slow to recover.

The other side of the same coin is literal non-reaction—not that the person has been ludicrously deflated by the event—but that the event does not seem to register or takes an absurdly long time to do so. A pedestrian notices a car driven by a dog go by, continues walking for a number of seconds, and then stops as "he gets it". We are talking, of course, of the famous double take. Someone has been unconsciously so psychically paralyzed by what has happened that they cannot respond in the normal reaction time. They must first deny what they have just seen by suddenly starting to sleepwalk—until the initial wildly disorienting impression has safely passed—and only then awaken to the truth. (Deadpan humor has been a classic staple in the repertoire of great comedians from Jack Benny (most famously with his chin cupped in his palm); Sid Caesar, with his pain double takes to Bill Cosby ("Hello, All The People"). By contrast, Woody Allen introduced what one might call the antithesis to the deadpan: the neurotic overreaction which, in his hands, became perhaps even funnier. Undoubtedly the most celebrated case of a television program being predicated on the single premise of just how inadvertently funny real life deadpan can be was Candid Camera: during which the reaction of unsuspecting, everyday people to secretly rigged, mind-boggling events—e.g., the soup spoon on a diner counter magically evading the grasp of a hungry customer—were stealthily videotaped, to be revealed with the ultimate punch line, "Smile, you're on Candid Camera").

Now what the person does who plays deadpan is to take this model and reverse it: by seemingly showing remarkably little responsiveness to what moves the other—without, however, revealing why they are not responding or that they may be incapable of doing so in any genuine way—the joke is at the other's expense. Except the joke is one of silent ridicule, which is then disavowed (here the analogy ends). The result of which is to turn the tables on the other, converting them from someone who thought they were about to really warm up their listener with their contagious enthusiasm to someone who dismally fails to do so: the psychic equivalent of putting a key in a car ignition which does not start.

It is obvious this is a maneuver that almost anyone can do with impunity. Although we are socially required to politely acknowledge the presence of another into whose company we have been introduced, we are under no obligation to reciprocate their enthusiasm, mirror their involvement or share in any way the meaningfulness of their personal experience. And even in instances of the almost universally recognized human tragedy—the unexpected death of a loved one—the most that is required is a brief and simple, "I'm sorry", followed by an appropriately sorrowful look. It is not even necessary that the look be genuine, only that it appear that way: that is, the other can have no feelings of real empathy so long as he or she is not observed in some fashion to be displaying obvious disrespect for the mourner's loss. Another way to put this, is that on the rare occasion of unquestionable tragedy the other is not allowed to be comfortably indifferent, but has to make at least a modest, bona fide attempt to be empathic. No more is expected.

And that is the point. In almost all interpersonal exchanges someone is free to exercise their supposedly autonomous right to be as indifferent, turned off, unempathic and unreciprocal as the case may be. To protest this, as already mentioned, is typically to provoke a culturally reinforced resistance to the effect that the other is trying to tell the person how to think, how to feel, how to behave.

Therein lies the considerable potential for someone who chooses to act deadpan—without, of course, letting the other know that it is a strategy—to disorient and disrupt the rhythm of the other's being. And since the other cannot effectively protest or even be sure whether or not the person is truly indifferent to their efforts at self-expression—yet do not themselves have the option to be similarly immune (although this is characteristically what they will try to simulate) to the person's indifference—they thereby become vulnerable to any apparent subtext of indifference. It follows that the opportunities for anyone who wants to manipulate such subtexts of deadpan indifference—essentially, for example, by merely feigning a lack of interest, regardless of how they feel, in order to produce an immediate deflating impact on the other—are almost limitless.

BEING THE STRAIGHT MAN

An obvious variation on the above, might be called playing the straight man: refusing to take any responsibility for investing one's emotions in the interaction at hand—in order to shift the burden for kindling interpersonal enthusiasm upon the other—by unconsciously pretending as though one earnestly believes that it is this other who has something to say.

As the example of comedy shows, the straight man is someone who unobtrusively but quite smoothly leads the star comic—through deceptively innocent questions and deftly timed nonchalance—to the hidden punch line: no small part of the comedy—in addition to the potential punch line payoff—is the short-sighted, robotic literal-mindedness and exaggerated dumbness of the designated straight man which serves as the ideal foil to the comic's triumphant cleverness. The skill of the straight man is therefore twofold: to set up the punch line by maintaining an offsetting, methodical pace and to divert attention away from guessing what is to come, by lulling the audience with their unimaginative lack of comprehensive (reminiscent of what Freud once said about the mechanism of hypnotism: to bore the subject's consciousness so as to allow the unconscious to take over).

When, however, used as a real life power game, the joke, of course, is on the other and there is nothing funny about it. The interpersonal straight man then is someone who unconsciously gauges what would be a meaningful, reciprocal response—what the other would most likely require in order to have the substance of what they are saying satisfactorily mirrored—and then plays dumb—not in the sense of deadpan—but by acting as though whatever is of import is yet to come. Another way to say this is that to play the straight man in the realm of unconscious communication is to deny that a psychological punch line has been delivered.

By pretending not to "get" their unconscious drift, the other is immediately placed into a double bind: on the one hand, they can not receive any validation from the straight man because they are aware that—from the perspective of their true self—for some reason they have decidedly fallen flat; on the other hand, it is exceedingly difficult to call into question the lack of receptivity of a person who, to all intents and purposes, appears to be still earnestly listening, still ready to receive the payoff which he has not heard or not understood. The effect, of course, is to frustrate the other who is now driven to either repeat the original message (which, typically, meets the same fate) or accept their failure at self-expression. (These dynamics are similar to those of what I call the withholding personality (Alper, 1996), someone who is adept at making another feel like he is "waiting for Godot").

Finally, it is easy to be the straight man inasmuch as: the need for an unconscious message (as Christopher Bollas calls it, "news from the self") to be received will usually be greater on the part of the one who has gone to the trouble of composing it, than on the part of the listener who has no such investment at stake. Accordingly, it will require little effort and less risk to elect not to become engaged with the person's expressive acts (for example, compare the time it takes a practiced editor—estimated to be an average of about fifteen seconds—to decide whether or not to accept a particular manuscript with the time it takes (often years) to originate and shape a serious idea for a book). And therein lies its effectiveness as a power game.

THE DENIAL OF MEANING

Yet another variation of deadpan and straight man, this may be the simplest power game of all to play.

All someone has to do is:

1. Relate as though everything—but personal meaning—is being communicated: information, gossip, know-how, feeling states, social pleasantries and so on.

2. Meaning is denied by reacting as though what is at stake in the communication of the other is only of functional, pragmatic or transient value. Thus, even if the news is not good, the receptive attitude that is adopted can still be one of relatively bland concern mixed with tepid optimism: e.g., news of having just lost one's job can be greeted with bromides, "Maybe it's for the best" ... Hallmark-card sympathy, "It's harder looking for a job than getting one" ... or a version of Eric Berne's famous game, "Ain't it awful". In short, the person makes

sure that depth of true feeling is not tapped and that, whenever there is a need, the subject can be changed without much fanfare.

It follows that the basic unconscious strategy for denying meaning is twofold: to deliberately fail to mirror meaning in whatever the other is expressing, and to fail to allow meaning to be evoked in the listener.

When this occurs, the denial of meaning is tantamount to the denial of the presence of the true self.

HOLDING ON

This could be to almost any constellation of hurt feelings: to anger, a grudge, a narcissistic injury and so on.

The dynamics of why this can be a winning strategy are:

1. By freezing the particular interpersonal point of view one wants to cultivate, one automatically imposes a biased interpretation that cannot be reciprocally shared. One, thereby, so to speak, chooses the emotional playing field.

2. Holding on breaks the flow of spontaneous interaction. It keeps the future at bay by insuring that the past is relived.

3. Holding on can provide a false sense that you are being serious and standing behind what you say, as though the reason you are refusing to move on is that you are committed to following through with the consequences of what you feel (the other, by comparison, can seem fickle and lacking the courage to face the music).

4. Holding on may create the impression, or contribute to the fantasy that you are not someone to be trifled with, a sleeping lion not to be aroused, that you do not bear insults lightly.

Perhaps the best example of the effectiveness of such a strategy is the person who does not let go of their anger. This works if only because the realization that someone's anger is actually a long term affair, with no end in sight—and not something that, as is usually the case, tends to dissipate upon being discharged—is in itself quite intimidating. As though he or she has access to a weapon—a seemingly unlimited store of unused anger—that can be unsheathed at any time. Holding on means, of course, that the fate of the anger—in spite of the fact it involves another—lies solely in the hands of the person. For the one holding on to the anger, it can thereby seem as though a balance is being struck between doing something that is dangerous—kindling one's anger instead of tempering it—yet somehow maintaining control—holding back as well as holding on—with the net effect that one feels safely stimulated.

From such a perspective, keeping the anger going can be seen as a defense against an accompanying, underlying and frustrated sense of something being held back (due either to an inability or fear of releasing it). To continue to kindle one's anger is to return to an emotion that may partly have spent itself. By zealously endeavoring to spark it to life, as though one can not get enough of it, the unconscious message is sent that one can not only tolerate but requires more action and more heat. What typically, and deliberately, gets overlooked is the troubling fact that--to continue the metaphor—the embers of anger can neither die out nor catch fire on their own account but seem to demand a conscientious and artificial tending

PAYBACK

This is an obvious derivative of the above, which to a certain extent has been glorified in our pop culture. The strategic advantages which it seems to offer are:

1. You do not relate to the uncertain, spontaneous present and future. What anger you do have in the present is to a remembered injustice in the past upon which you have passed judgment. You are therefore clear as to the amount of retaliation that is appropriate and are in a position—rare in cases of here and now, reactive annoyance—to measure the quantity of anger to be released.

By contrast, your target is placed at an immediate disadvantage: sensing that you are responding to the memory of a former slight that is incomparably more vivid and meaningful to you than to them, they will realize that—in order to put up an adequate defense—they will, so to speak, have to catch up. That is, reconstruct the probable cause of your original narcissistic injury—to determine the extent to which you may be overreacting—so as to decide how best to respond.

2. It follows someone who is engaged in payback is likely to feel in charge. After all, the occasion for comeuppance will be opportunistically selected—which means he will enjoy the added advantage of initiating an act of retribution at a time when the other will be in the kind of dependent or weakened position that does lend itself to self-defense.

3. Not surprisingly, no small part of the pleasure of payback is that it is frankly punitive: it is intended to be and usually is viewed by its target as patently unfair—coming as it does when they are not prepared to fight back—and is thereby supposed—by the law of the talon (eye for an eye, tooth for a tooth)—to remind the other of the injustice they originally visited upon the person, an injustice that is now being repaid. What payback thus unconsciously aims at is a *parity of victimization:* to induce in the other a persecutory paranoia that, paradoxically, may facilitate a kind of symbiotic communication.

Payback, thus, originates from a paranoid position: the gnawing belief that the other is so immune to one's pain and suffering that only through an act of identification can he or she understand. The unconscious formula at work here is if paranoia = a belief in the persecutor's malignant absence of empathy, then the persecutor can only understand if he *becomes* paranoid himself; and this means learning is only possible by transforming the perceived oppressor into a clone of oneself. In short: payback = the unconscious attempt to coerce identification as a necessary substitute for what is seen as a failure of ordinary learning through communication and empathy.

4. The drawback is that there is no future. If what you're into is settling the score, it is what has happened that is exciting not what can happen (other than the consummatory act of revenge, with its accompanying illusion of undoing the past). From the standpoint of the intended victim, however, it is especially demoralizing to realize that someone who is bent upon justice at your expense, must feel quite hopeless about the future of the relationship.

5. On the other hand, payback can represent for the avenger-to-be a second chance, a wiping the slate clean, the removal of a lingering shame and therefore can also seem a kind of tough-love version of optimism. Such a person may imagine they are even teaching the other a much needed lesson (in accordance with the logic of Hamlet: "I must be cruel, only to be kind"). And when this is the case, he or she—secretly believing that "You'll thank me for this one day"—may even look for signs of possible gratitude.

6. Again, by contrast, the other will understandably have a decidedly unempathic view of the act of payback when it arrives. Typically it will be regarded as devious (if the grievance were an honest one, why was it kept under wraps so carefully?); cowardly (why else would it come as a Pearl Harbor-like attack?); and mean-spirited (why does it have to be delivered in the guise of a vindictive lesson?). Whatever trust existed prior to the payback, therefore, tends to get destroyed. Which means—what to someone who considers himself to have been wronged and who believes he is delivering a long-overdue lesson—may well be, from the standpoint of the victim, proof that the person is intent on totally alienating them.

For all of these reasons, the other will often feel deeply disrespected, betrayed, unloved and toyed with. If there is a so-called lesson to be learned, it is to not leave oneself vulnerable to payback in the future. From the victim's perspective, the severity of animosity revealed in the act of getting even can be used as a yardstick to measure the degree of previously unexpressed anger. (Because it has hitherto been so secretive and guarded, the release of this type of anger is especially scary: unconsciously it is felt that the person must be frightened of it, too, otherwise, why bury it?)

Finally, by introducing the leitmotif of revenge, payback—as a secondary benefit—brings in the element of mystery and the corresponding need for detective work. For in order to carry on a relationship, while concealing that one is intending to settle an old score, it will be necessary to be not only careful but suspicious of what the other is thinking (as Adam Phillips has cannily noted in another context, 1995—"philosophers love suspicion—there is something to know, something worth knowing"). There are other advantages, too. As an unconscious theme, the aim of revenge can organize into a cohesive, reality-based plot what may otherwise be experienced as a disturbing, diffuse, internal rage. To plot revenge means that one has automatically added the factor of dynamic time. The time that is added is not just any time—not time in the abstract—but narrative, dramatic time. Which means time that is timed to deliver a very specific and complex emotional jolt.

And thereby powerful justification has been found for postponing the release of rage: to make it subordinate to an overall plan to which is attributed a central meaning. Rage that had previously been amorphous and directionless is now placed into a narrative framework and made linear. What may have rankled and felt like raw hatred has been made instrumental—its purpose now being to advance the action of the revenge fantasy.

Before, when it was the other way around, it seemed like rage was calling the shots—a ticking bomb looking for a trigger to explode it—in which case the psyche-soma was reduced to the subservient role of being merely the container or releaser of the central event which was the explosion to come. It is just this seductive promise of a transformation of perplexing inner rage into a titillating and winnable game that makes the prospect of payback so inviting.

DUELING NARCISSISTS

When two people—who unfortunately for one reason or another happen to be at their most fragile—are interacting, the outcome can be characterized as the antithesis of mutuality and empathic interrelating. In short, a congruence of fragility produces what is known as bad chemistry.

Typically, then, the relationship begins to rapidly deteriorate. There is an escalation of negative distancing. In a paranoid way, the other's neediness is perceived as a dangerously intrusive demand, as the person unconsciously realizes he or she cannot possibly meet it and that such refusal is likely to be viewed as a further narcissistic injury. Which in turn precipitates an incipient panic that there will be a hostile and aggressive increase in demands. To counter this, the person, in a preemptive strike, may decide to present his or her own psychic bill of grievances. Not surprisingly, this is often greeted in an analogously paranoid way as a menacing intrusion and what results is a competition or duel to determine whose demands are going to prevail. This usually takes the form—literally—of person A, announcing his demand, immediately followed by person B, thrusting forward her demand, during which it becomes uncomfortably and increasingly evident that there is not likely to be the slightest attempt by either party to address, let alone meet, the other's need. A typical transaction of this kind—perhaps best illustrated in a lover's quarrel—may go like this.

He: Lately, you've become more and more self-involved and pay less and less attention to me.

She: Nothing I say or do ever satisfies you.

He: That's a great example of what I mean. I tell you you've been ignoring me lately and your response is that what you want is for me to be less critical of you.

She: Well, you're criticizing me right now, aren't you?

He: No, you're focusing on yourself right now and not paying any attention to what I'm legitimately complaining about.

She: That's what I mean. You're always legitimately complaining.
He: And you're always telling me what you need and what you're not getting.
She: Is there any point to this?
He: Unless I'm giving you exactly what you think you want, I guess not.

It is obvious the transaction goes nowhere: either repeating itself with obsessive competitiveness or petering out, at which point both parties withdraw—considerably more exhausted and demoralized than before the duel began—to silently survey the extent of their fresh narcissistic injury. It follows the aftermath of this kind of duel will tend to be negatively reinforcing. What commences in a state of mutual mistrust ends with an even greater conviction on behalf of each party that they will have to fight if their needs are going to be met.

In such a scenario, not only is the possibility of empathy for the other inhibited, it is fair to say it is poisoned. The genuine needs of the other become—instead of aspects of the true self with which to resonate—agents of oppression. The other then is someone who is making demands—not to remedy a neglected although a bona fide deficit—but as a tactic for persecuting the person. And when the duel reaches a fever pitch, as it often does, the demands are perceived as toxic intrusions posing as individual grievances.

How does a demand get perceived as a toxic intrusion? Foremost, by being decontextualized: now there is no time, before and after, no developmental process preceding the need, in particular, no ambient self. By contrast, the need is viewed as almost distilled greed, as ravenous hunger, and the demand to be fed is experienced as a form of blackmail: "I won't stop pestering you, until you feed me."

From this standpoint, dueling narcissists are unconsciously engaged in a territorial fight over who has begging rights. Such a duel at bottom is a mini tantrum, with the infantilism covered up by the aggressive invasiveness: that is, the illusion is fostered that one is taking rather than begging. The tantrum, then, can be seen as a manifestation of aggressive, explosive infantilism and the tantrum-thrower as someone who projects his neediness into the other by upsetting her with his list of impossible demands. In this fashion, she is painted into a defensive corner—one she needs to get out of if she is to restore her belief in her autonomy (it is the perception of this dilemma by the would-be power player that engenders a false sense of winning).

Finally, it is no accident that the demands that are made by dueling narcissists characteristically verge on the impossible: their hugeness is felt necessary by the person to effectively disarm and bully the other. And in order not to feel deprived, the distraught person feels compelled to transform his or her needs into weapons.

"JUST THE FACTS"

As a psychotherapist, I cannot help but be intrigued by relationship experts—who make a point of appearing regularly on radio and TV—and who all offer, to a greater or lesser extent, immediate solutions to complex life problems.

To take just one of countless examples, there is the cable television program I recently saw. The host was a late night star (I'll call him Sammy) and the show was billed as a presumably earnest discussion of conflict resolution. The featured guest was a best-selling psychologist who radiated total self-assurance. In his opening monologue, Sammy, who was fond of adopting oppositional stances in regard to his guests, stated that it was often dangerous to express one's negative feelings, especially to one's closest family members. "What if they take offense, and never see you again?" Sammy asked with a solemn look.

The unflappable psychologist smiled good-naturedly at the host's contrariness. "Sammy, you seem to think confrontation means to clash, but it simply means facing something or someone."

Sammy held his ground. "But what if you tell a family member something as honestly as you can and they still refuse to listen to you?"

This time, the response of the psychologist was gentle and serious. "Sometimes, all you can have with a toxic relative is what I call a parlor relationship."

Without bothering to acknowledge the reply, Sammy changed the subject. "What do you do, if someone keeps abusing you? How do you get them to stop, short of slugging them, which is my impulse?"

The psychologist peered into the camera. It was a question she appeared eager to answer. "First, you recognize that you are in an abusive relationship. Then you have to be firm, even tough if necessary, about getting out of it. I recommend saying, "You have verbal BO, so I won't stick around!"

Sammy, who plainly liked this response, was warming to the conversation. "But what if they come back--and believe me, this has happened to me more than once--and say you're just being thin-skinned?"

Unfazed, the psychologist seemed to set her jaw as she made her reply. "Then I say, 'Maybe, I am thin-skinned, but now that I've told you, we both know that if you do it again—it'll be because you want to abuse me!"

From the standpoint of our theme, what is of interest is that a long-standing, psychic conflict is treated as a simple instance of a lack of information. As though all that is required is for them to be told what a healthy person would do in their situation, and they can do it. It is conveniently overlooked that they typically are not presenting themselves as an especially mature, healthy person and the reason they are not behaving in such a fashion is that they need for an underlying dysfunction to be treated first.

It is therefore an easy way to dismiss someone who is suffering from an unresolved, genuine conflict by acting as though what is necessary is advice, information or perhaps some high-powered cognitive strategies. To make my point clearer, I suggest the (admittedly polemical) analogy of a fever: it is as though someone—instead of seeing the high temperature as an obvious symptom of an underlying illness—is regarding it as the manifestation of a dearth of information: i.e., someone with fever is merely ignorant of how an individual with a normal temperature behaves and conducts his life and so—if you describe the behavior of a normal person—they will begin to get better to the degree they emulate healthy activities.

By implicitly claiming that facts are what is needed, the allegation is made that ignorance is at the root of the problem; furthermore, that there is no longer any excuse—short of laziness or downright malingering—for not correcting the problem now that the missing data has been supplied. Thus facts take on a moral, didactic tone, as though they are offered in the spirit of teaching or of being helpful (on the contrary, they are often a means, especially when given as a substitute for relating, of appearing superior: to cover up an inability to respond in an empathic, reciprocal fashion).

There is a sense in which teaching—by creating an almost immediate, hierarchical relationship—can be a strategy to avoid relating. After all, the traditional teacher-student dyad, by definition, is asymmetrical. There is someone who knows something worth knowing and someone who presumably does not know it, but may need to. Only one person is in possession of what both agree is the primary object of their interaction.

It follows, however, that although both may gain satisfaction from the transaction, it cannot be the same satisfaction. To teach therefore is to instate a difference—supposedly the result of dissimilar life experience—between the two participants. In a subtle way, the putative teacher places the other in a double bind: on the one hand, the manifest inequity in cognitive achievement is supposedly being rectified in an egalitarian fashion by a redistribution of the available store of knowledge; on the other hand, the very activity of teaching is a powerful reinforcer of the student's ignorance and, at least while operant, can serve to keep him in his place. Or, to put it another way, the student is only allowed to stay in his place to the extent that he stays in his place.

If the currency of the interpersonal exchange is defined as knowledge and the value of the exchange is to be based on the accuracy or usefulness of such knowledge, then the behavior of the teacher is of secondary importance and this means—providing there are no outright abuses stemming from the considerably greater authority inhering in the expert status of the teacher (or from student rebelliousness that has gotten out of hand)—the relationship per se will not be held accountable and no particular meaning, other than a functional one, will be attached to it.

Instead, meaning is attributed to the exploration and discovery of knowledge. The act of teaching, as mentioned, implies that there is something worth knowing, something worth doing that has not yet been done, and that there is something better to do than staying pat in the present situation (knowledge as pointing to the future, to a vista that lies beyond psychic space).

On the everyday interpersonal plane, therefore, one way to disempower and devalue the other is to provide facts—as a substitute for relating—and useful information—as a proxy for meaning.

The dispensing of information as a strategy for control, however, is by no means restricted to celebrity experts, to teachers, and to everyday power players. As the next chapter shows, it can even flourish in the heart of the mental health profession.

CHAPTER THREE

When Therapy Becomes A Power Struggle

I have already written (Alper, 1998) how therapy is supposed to be built on trust, collaboration and the making of a new kind of therapeutic relationship leading to greater insight and a broader perspective. Even more important for promoting the necessary trust than the esteem in which the patient holds the therapist (the positive transference) is what has been called the real relationship. This relationship will be closer to what is usually meant by the term 'therapeutic personality' and will have little to do with professional technique as such and will be based instead on what is perceived as being actually there and, especially, as worthy of being trusted. What, of course, will stand in the way of this kind of a genuinely trustworthy real relationship being established—upon which, with the help of legitimate technique, a therapeutic relationship can be facilitated—is the traditionally formidable, hierarchical and non-reciprocal structure of the artificial therapeutic situation. Not surprisingly, this will prove fertile soil for the power games we have been describing, to which we now turn. First, on the part of the therapist:

"IT'S FOR YOUR OWN GOOD"

If the behavior of the therapist is viewed as truly altruistically intended, it is difficult to hold him or her accountable for unavoidable, occasional mistakes. To do so, in fact, might seem ungrateful for everything that has been done in the past. Therapists who unconsciously wish to take advantage of the defense of altruism can do so by systematically de-emphasizing everything that might be seen as materialistic and self-serving about their chosen profession.

Thus the decor of the office—no matter how fancy, prestigious and Park Avenue-like—is typically arranged as though in the service of creating the best therapeutic milieu, and never for the purpose of presenting the most attractive and marketable image possible of the therapist. And when it comes to the finances of therapy, therapists will often discuss sensitive issues regarding even flagrant abuses of the contractual agreement regarding the fee (that cannot help personally affecting them)—for example, consistently late or delinquent payment—as but one more symptom of the dysfunctional behavior for which the patient came to treatment in the first place and for which he or she is presumably being treated. By that logic, the therapist who points out to his patient that she is being irresponsible by falling so far into arrears, is primarily treating the patient and only secondarily trying to collect on an unpaid bill. Should the therapist, however, be challenged on just this matter—that when they dun their patients for unpaid bills, they are acting out of financial self-interest—he will most likely concede that he is only a professional who provides a service for a fee, but he will tend to pass quickly over the point, as though--other than being an economic necessity that occasionally has to be dealt with--it is an unwelcome intrusion into the real purpose of the work that is taking place and far beneath it in terms of meaning and personal value.

By contrast, in real life therapists are often painfully divided and confused as to the extent that they are working for the fee or for the benefit of the patient. A good question to ask, then, is to what degree does the so-called art of psychotherapy represent a business to them? And to what extent do the prestige and social advantages that adhere to the status of mental health professional and expert drive them in their work? These ambiguities are intensified by what I have called the double bind nature of therapy (*Portrait of the Artist as a Young Patient*, Alper, 1997): the irreconcilable conflict arising in a craft such as psychotherapy that depends heavily on two intrinsically incompatible ingredients: technique and intimacy. Power games invariably develop when the therapist—instead of squarely facing his personal conflict over double bind issues—tries either to deny or use them to his own advantage.

There may be, for example, the therapist who, say, bored with himself, his work or his particular patient cannot wait for the hour to end so that he may more fully address his own feelings of deprivation. His greatest interest therefore is— not in the profundities of the psyche of the patient with whom he is professionally engaged—but in how much longer he must wait before the session is to end. His dilemma as a therapist then is that to reveal or act out his true state of mind would institute a breach of professional conduct gross enough to approach malpractice: that is, to stare pointedly at his watch—a faux pas in even the most trivial of social encounters—to a vulnerable patient who has been invited to and is presumably struggling to bare her soul, would be an unpardonable betrayal of trust. So it is obvious that a therapist whose dearest wish is to watch the clock, cannot do so. What is less obvious, is not immediately discernible and is often not faced, is that afterwards the bored therapist has a clear and compelling choice: he can take responsibility for his lack of interest, explore its dynamic meaning and reevaluate, if necessary, his suitability for this particular patient or for the profession as a whole; or he can simply ignore it, well aware that in order to escape detection in the future, all he has to do is maintain his customary professional demeanor: e.g., not to stare fixedly, but only occasionally steal glances at his watch, as do almost all therapists, and thereby keep his boredom to himself. (For what it is worth, I have never heard a therapist candidly discuss or even acknowledge their boredom or possible imminent burnout).

The other side of the coin of minimizing his professional and personal narcissistic self-interest, is to exaggerate his altruism. Thus, therapists regularly unconsciously over-identify with the built-in empathic, nurturing and ascetic features of their role: they subtly begin to believe or act as though they are a person who never raises their voice, loses their temper, becomes visibly distracted, preoccupied, behaves aggressively, intrusively, manipulatively, or interrupts the conversation because of a need to eat or go to the bathroom. In short, the therapist conducts himself—at least for the duration of the session—as though there is no object of greater interest in the universe than the vicissitudes of the patient's psyche. Although on the one hand, both patient and therapist can and do justify such a profoundly non-reciprocal interaction as being something mandated by the exigencies of the therapeutic frame, there is another sense—apropos of R.D. Laing's shrewd observation in *Self and Other* (1961) that "it's okay to imagine you're someone other than you are, provided you do not begin to believe it"—in which the therapist can begin to assume that his saintlike and discreetly glorious, therapeutic persona is but the professional expression of a truly high-minded and heroically self-denying human being. And from that standpoint, the traditional guarding of the therapist's private life and concentrated attempt to create a mysterious, neutral personality is as much an endeavor to prevent the illusion of a magically lofty, psychically pure creature being shattered—by allowing into the session all the non-therapeutic, narcissistic, conflictual, defensive, neurotic and false self elements existing in everyone but which have been carefully censored by the demands of the therapist's blank screen—as it is to maintain the appropriate boundaries between professional and personal life (once again, supposedly, for the patient's own good).

To put it another way, a common power game unconsciously played by therapists is to act as though their therapeutic self were essentially the same as their real self (which, of course, is impossible). Which does not mean that their real self is antithetical to their professional self (although, in some cases, unfortunately it is). It does mean that the real self in even the best therapist will contain parts that are essentially indifferent to the needs of the patient. From this it follows that many of the profoundest needs of the therapist's real self will have nothing to do with the needs of the patient.

The therapist, therefore, even if possessing a genuinely therapeutic personality—someone who is fundamentally kind, nurturing, empathic and thoughtful—will be much less that way in the course of his everyday, non-professional encounters with others. (Consider the analogy with a neurosurgeon:

although his hands are admittedly steady all day long, it is only during surgery that they approach their famously golden, God-like lightness of touch).

To sum up: the natural altruistic bent of the therapist becomes contaminated and opportunistically exploited when it is presented—not simply as a requirement of the role—but as akin to a sacred personal identity.

"I USED TO BE JUST LIKE YOU"

A popular companion game to the above is the assumption that—while the therapist certainly does share a common humanity with even the most profoundly dysfunctional patient and is vulnerable to the same tendencies to neurotic or even psychotic behavior—whatever personal conflicts did develop have been resolved most likely years before the present patient showed up. It is implied, therefore, that what the therapist can offer, in addition to his or her technical expertise, is the inspirational presence of an authentic mental health role model.

There are certain ways by which the therapist may attempt to indicate that—unlike the patient before him—he has achieved lasting mental health:

1. He can deport himself with the kind of uncanny self-control that is simply not seen anywhere else in everyday society: whatever needs he has being so well managed that they are never brought up and rarely seem to obtrude themselves. Such self-control that is evidenced by unconscious inference is linked to the operation of a strong and efficient ego, one that has presumably at least learned how to keep maladaptive defenses in check.

2. He can as a rule act unthreatened and even in harmony with the great unknown. Phrases such as, "I can't say" ... "We'll have to explore that", sprinkle his conversation. Paradoxically, the impression is given that he is so confident of what he does know, that he can embrace in a spirit of adventurous exploration the realm of his uncertainty. Thus, the therapist cannot lose: he is wise enough to know what he knows and wise enough to know when he does not know.

3. The therapist can and usually does choose not to flinch in the presence of the illness, no matter how ominous, that the patient brings into the consulting room. While he will often make a point of asserting he cannot read the patient's mind, is in no way a psychic when it comes to assaying future outcomes, he will almost never admit to being inadequate to the task at hand, to not having at least a professionally plausible idea—no matter how intractable the problem—on how best to proceed.

To the extent that this, of course, is what we come to experts for, what we insist they give us—a deft, seemingly magical surehandedness in the face of what to everyone else would be Gordian knots—we overlook the grandiosity that we thereby project upon them. For it is simply impossible for ordinary mortals—regardless of how steeped they may be in a certain know-how—to be able to predictably cope with the vast and unimaginable contingencies intrinsic to the complexities of human relations. And while it is understandable that patients will often transferentially deny the many limitations of what their therapy has to offer, it is less forgivable that their therapists will choose to collude by playing the role of the ubiquitous expert who hasn't seen a conflict he can't confidently tackle.

Yet, it is just this that many therapists do: in spite of stock disclaimers that they don't have the answers—"You have to decide"—they make a point of never conceding defeat in the sense of admitting they are not a suitable therapist for this particular patient; of never showing real confusion, resignation, frustration or anger at the obstacles to progress in the treatment. Whatever their patient does—skip sessions, fall asleep, decline to pay, abuse, ridicule and compete with the therapist at every turn—they must go out of their way not to appear disappointed.

To sum up, the unconscious message in the case where the aim is to obtain power, is that although the mental health professional may be ignorant in areas that lie outside of his domain of competence, there is really nothing he does not know that he needs to know in order to enact his role as expert. (In this regard, see especially Adam Phillip's wonderful treatment of the subject in *Terrors and*

Experts, 1996; or, for a much fuller discussion of my own views, *The Dark Side of the Analytic Moon*, Alper, 1996).

We now turn to some games patients play.

"I'M NOT GETTING ANY BETTER"

1. It is commonplace for patients to confuse the end goal with the means, overlooking that the process of psychotherapy is one of flux, entailing ebb and flow. Since, however, ours is a high-tech, information-exchange culture, in which progress is measured in a quantitative and linear fashion, this can subtly put instant pressure on the therapist to be productive in a similar fashion. The unconscious message becomes: if psychotherapy is a service for a fee, then that service is a product, and if a product, its benefits should be tangible and quantifiable.

2. The patient thus shifts the responsibility for getting better entirely onto the shoulders of the therapist, thereby robbing him of the primary raw material with which he works—the patient's motivation.

3. The therapist is placed into an immediate double bind: if he accepts the patient's assessment—that he or she does not seem to be getting any better—he is also accepting the covert allegation of deficient treatment; if he questions it, he runs the risk of appearing defensive in a self-serving way. At the same time, however, it is almost impossible for the responsible mental health professional to become—if not somewhat defensive—then at least concerned for the continuity of the therapy. For, typically, the next step after the vocal complaint of a clear lack of progress, is the lessening of interest in the treatment, to be succeeded by a noticeable withdrawal and followed, sooner or later, by a decision to terminate therapy.

4. The therapist is thus forced to act—instead of to interact.

5. A classic counter move now on the part of the therapist who wishes to extricate himself from this dilemma is to respond with the mildly confrontive

interpretation that perhaps the patient may not be working hard enough to achieve the results that he or she expects. Since more often than not there are clinical grounds for assuming that this is the case, the beleaguered therapist may feel he is after all only doing his job by thereby shifting at least some of the responsibility for making progress back onto the patient.

But it is obvious that one problem with such a tactic is the therapist may unwittingly lapse into playing—"It's for your own good". And on some level the patient will probably realize this: since the unconscious purpose of playing—"I'm not getting any better"—to a large extent is to contend with the therapist, perhaps even getting the best of him, the patient will be on the lookout for signs of any uncharacteristic lack of poise, self-consciousness and, especially, defensiveness. (It is worth noting, one of the most passionate and successful forms of unconscious communication is between defense and defense, and false self to false self. The basic dynamics of which are: (1) A has a (defensive) need to find a chink in B's psychic armor and is thereby motivated to conduct a diligent search, knowing that it will only be a matter of time before one of B's primary defense mechanisms will make an appearance; (2) once this happens A will most likely test the new hypothesis, that one of B's defenses has been discovered, by challenging it (analogous to putting slight pressure on an area suspected of pain, to confirm that one has located a context of inordinate psychic sensitivity, one merely introduces a little stress and then waits for the reaction); (3) should the hypothesis be verified, A will begin to observe even more closely the vicissitudes of B's defensiveness in order to find out how best to take advantage of it, and one of the most opportune times will be when she needs to; that is (4) when A herself is feeling too vulnerable for comfort and thereby could use some extra leverage; (5) and by such time will have presumably grown hyper-vigilant vis-á-vis signs of B's defensiveness and is hardly likely to miss them.)

6. Compounding matters is that the therapist on some level may be aware of his countertransferential wish to play—"It's for your own good". At this juncture, however, it is usually too difficult to stop in mid-game and work on his

personal issues. And what happens instead is that the therapist begins to force the interaction: trying to make whatever defensive point he wants to make quickly so as to end the game, which itself has become a cause of anxiety, as soon as possible. (It is worth noting that it is always hard to tell, when someone is being defensive, what it is they are warding off—the original fear or the equally anxiety-producing and always present possibility of a malfunctioning of the specific defensive operation: defenses, after all, among other things, are encoded containers of negative memories and affects).

7. In turn, the patient, who has been both suspecting and hoping for signs of the above, will feel validated in his perception that the therapist is defensively playing, "It's for your own good". And finally, this will be damning evidence and explanation of why he is not getting any better, reinforcing the need for distance and defensive self-preservation.

USING THE THERAPIST

Winnicott (1971) has written profoundly from a developmental standpoint concerning the vicissitudes of object use by the infant and Christopher Bollas (1987) has brilliantly expanded that concept by applying it to the various transferential enactments of adult patients in psychoanalysis. By contrast, I am limiting the employment of the concept—to highlight the power operations that are latent in its defensive expression—to the pejorative sense, aptly denoted in the vernacular complaint, "I feel used".

It is obvious that use here really means abuse: to a greater or lesser extent, the person may feel used up, mistreated, objectified, hoodwinked, manipulated, toyed with. Typically, such an assessment is retrospectively arrived at. Someone feels used when: it dawns on them that almost none of their expectations have been realized; that they have essentially been engaged in a non-reciprocal transaction that has brought benefit only to the other, and that they have to some degree been actively misled into believing that the other had some different purpose in mind than simply exploiting them. As a consequence, however, they may then feel morally superior to the one who has used them, entitled, therefore, to use them back and well warned never to make the mistake of trusting the other again.

Using the therapist can be employed as a power game by the patient who is so inclined in either a passive or an active fashion.

Passive: When the therapist is experienced unconsciously, and sometimes consciously—despite protestation to the contrary—as someone who is employing technique for his or her own benefit. Feeling thereby deprived and used, the patient can justifiably withdraw from the demands of the relationship or retaliate by seeking to use the therapist in turn.

Active: This is more common and generally occurs unconsciously. The patient, for a variety of defensive reasons, endeavors to use the therapeutic encounter primarily as a means for gratification. This can mean:

1. Trying to take charge: by, for example, complaining and asserting, "I'm not getting any better"; or by framing the therapeutic transaction as primarily and economic one: a service (the product) is being offered for a fee. Progress is then to be assessed in terms of product benefits or market value (to be determined, perhaps, by some healthy comparison shopping). From such a point of view, to complain about unsatisfactory benefits cannot be resistance, but is instead the exercise of the individual's right to stand behind one's beliefs and preferences.

2. As a corollary to the above, the way to approach one's therapy is pragmatically in terms of what works in the here and now. And, thus, brief psychotherapy, crisis intervention and medication—anything that promises a quick fix—begins to make sense as a treatment of choice.

3. Unconsciously there may be an automatic denial of meaning other than symptom alleviation. Using then represents an antithesis of coming to terms with long-term existential issues. What is important now becomes winning and losing, controlling or being controlled, and the goal of enhanced mental health is insidiously replaced by the wish to feel good.

To sum up, using, by definition, undercuts the possibility of engagement which is the linchpin of therapy. It then becomes a self-fulfilling prophecy: by applying power operations to the defenses of the therapist, it elicits guarded, self-involved behavior which, however altruistically framed, unconsciously reinforces the patient's perception that each of them is really in this for themselves (and so had better get the most out of it while they can). The implicit philosophy, in interpersonal terms, is to take the money and run. Finally, in using, the relationship becomes a contest, the other is viewed as an obstacle, cooperation switches to competition and respect gives way to wariness and a grudging appreciation of the other's ability to take advantage of the person.

CONCLUSION

Power games are rough-hewn psychodynamic strategies unconsciously enacted primarily to spare the person the imagined angst that would be stirred up by anything remotely approximating, at that particular dynamic moment in time, an authentic encounter. Although they can be characterological, they do not have to be: all people, even those rare individuals who are capable of ongoing intimacy, are forced at moments of frailty or interpersonal indecisiveness to play power games and certainly the culture at large pervasively sponsors the enactment of opportunistic interpersonal strategies.

Some of the more prevalent power games discussed are: to hold someone to public accountability in a way designed to prove shameful to them (by informing on them): to go by the book, performing a scripted role, devoid of spontaneity, in which interrelating is replaced by a series of well-practiced steps; to unconsciously emulate—when we have been challenged to explain our rationale for exercising some localized power which we have managed to acquire—the bullying tactics resorted to in moments of stress by our parents (culturally reinforced as "the voice of experience"); to stress our identification in the past ("I used to be that way") with what the other is presently undergoing, but as a covert way of deflecting attention away from our aim which is to manipulate the other into changing their behavior when they do not really intend to; to regard one's conversation, when there is a strong opportunistic motive for so doing, as a performance of a certain kind ("radio relating"); to approach a relationship from the standpoint of crisis intervention and appeal, not to the other's need for intersubjective enrichment, but to their sense of compassion for the downtrodden ("I have a lot of problems"); to achieve one-upmanship by putting the other on the defensive through calling attention to their somber, alarmed or needy state of mind—the undermining inference being that it is the person's failure to adapt, defend or adequately master that is at the root of the problem; negative closure; being impossible; being critical; being anxious; getting in the last word; the power of contempt; being bored; being condescending; the dynamics of power games; worshiping the power god within; strategies for winning; dropping the information bomb; providing useless information; muting the other; deadpan; playing the straight man; dueling narcissists; and when therapy becomes a power game.

To the power player relating is a game to be played and to be won. If success is to come from one's skill, and at the other's expense, it is necessary to learn the rules and the strategies that prevail—which always implies an abandonment or temporary suspension of one's investment in intimacy. There are literally thousands of such games played millions of times daily in America. This is because—and a major theme of this book—intimacy, being an intrinsically complex state of mind difficult to achieve, occurs rarely in our present day culture.

REFERENCES

Alper, G. (1993). "The Theory of Games and Psychoanalysis" *The Journal of Contemporary Psychotherapy*, 23(1):47-60.

Narcissistic Giving (1996). Bethesda, Maryland: International Scholars Publications.

The Dark Side of the Analytic Moon (1996). Bethesda, Maryland: International Scholars Publications.

Minding The Other's Mind: The Factor of Control in Contemporary Relationships (1997). Bethesda, Maryland: International Scholars Publications.

Portrait of the Artist as a Young Patient (1997). Bethesda, Maryland: International Scholars Publications.

Power Plays: Their Uses and Abuses in Human Relations (1998). Bethesda, Maryland: International Scholars Publications.

Berne, E. (1964). *Games People Play.* New York: Grove Press Inc.

Bion, W. R. (1967). *Second Thoughts.* New York: Jason Aronson.

Bollas, C. (1987). *The Shadow of the Object.* New York: W.W. Norton and Co.

Being a Character (1993). New York: Hill and Wang, a division of Farrar, Straus and Giroux.

Cracking Up (1995). New York: Hill and Wang.

Dennett, D. (1996). *Kinds of Minds.* New York: Basic Books.

Erikson, E. (1959). "Identity and The Life Cycle." *Psychological Issues*, No. 1, New York: International Universities Press.

Fairbairn (1952). "The Repression and Return of Bad Objects." In *Psychoanalytic Studies of the Personality*. London and New York: Routledge.

Farber, L. (1966). *Ways of the Will*. New York: Basic Books.

Freud, S. "On the Psychical Mechanism of Hysterical Phenomena: Preliminary Communication." Translated. Collected papers (5 Vols.) London, 1924-50.

Goffman, E. (1959). *Interaction Ritual*. New York: Pantheon.

Kohut, H. (1971). *The Analysis of the Self*. New York: International Universities Press.

Laing, R.D. (1961). *Self and Others*. London: Tavistock Publications.

Knots (1970). New York: Pantheon Books.

Phillips, A. (1994). *On Flirtation*. Cambridge, Massachusetts: Harvard University Press.

(1996). *Terrors and Experts*. Cambridge, Massachusetts: Harvard University Press.

(1998). *The Beast in the Nursery*. New York: Pantheon Books.

Sullivan, H.S. (1973). *Clinical Studies in Psychiatry*. New York: W.W. Norton.

Thomas, D. (1984). "Portrait of the Artist as a Young Dog" in *The Collected Stories*. New York: New Directions.

Winnicott, D.W. (1971). *Playing and Reality*. New York: Basic Books.

Wittgenstein, L. (1980). *Culture and Value*. Chicago: University of Chicago Press.

INDEX

A

abusive, 65, 112, 129
accountability, 6, 7, 66, 145
accusation, 6, 7, 12, 13, 14, 15, 40
accuser, 12, 13, 14, 15
active, 48, 142
addictive relating, 1
aggression, 65
Alper, Gerald, 34, 60, 85, 120, 133, 134, 139, 147
ambivalence, 22, 47, 97
amoral, 39
analogy of a fever, 129
anger, 14, 15, 23, 24, 39, 44, 49, 50, 88, 97, 121, 122, 124, 138
anti-identity, 16
anxiety, 39, 40, 44, 73, 74, 77, 78, 79, 80, 81, 82, 83, 84, 141
apprehension, 52, 73
atheism, 50
atmospheric danger, 80
audience, 33, 34, 58, 68, 113, 114, 119

B

Beast in the Nursery, 115, 148
behavioral puppetry, 1, 101
being discounted, 18
betrayal, 17, 37, 41, 49, 135
black box theory, 81
blackmail, 40, 127
blood pressure, 75, 76, 77
bodyguard, 102
Bollas, Christopher, 17, 35, 66, 67, 69, 87, 89, 96, 108, 120, 141, 147
book thief, 11
bored, 34, 92, 93, 95, 115, 135, 146
boredom, 91, 93, 94, 95, 135

by the book, 17, 18, 19, 20, 21, 23, 24, 31, 145

C

cancer, 73, 76, 77, 83
clinical psychologist, 59
clinical vignettes, 2
colonoscopy, 73, 75, 77, 78
communication, 33, 34, 57, 88, 91, 119, 120, 123, 124, 140
compartmentalization, 81, 83
compliance, 29, 101
concussion, 19
condescending, 11, 14, 95, 96, 99, 146
condescending manner, 11
contempt, 86
control, 19, 40, 41, 69, 79, 82, 90, 112, 122, 131, 137
counter strategy, 25
coward, 79
criminal prosecutor, 13
critiquing the other's emotive script, 114
crowd of fears, 82

D

daring assertiveness, 5
deadpan, 116
defense, 12, 15, 16, 22, 23, 40, 46, 51, 55, 65, 71, 80, 81, 82, 85, 90, 122, 123, 133, 140
defensive strategies, 15
denial, 16, 21, 24, 34, 49, 71, 72, 81, 90, 94, 121, 142
Dennett, Daniel, 108, 147
devious, 53, 55, 124

dilemma, 28, 34, 51, 108, 128, 135, 139
disclaimers, 65, 66, 138
dissent, 49
distrust, 19, 45
divorce, 41, 50
dynamic, 23, 34, 38, 40, 55, 71, 84, 101, 112, 125, 135, 145
dynamic interaction, 38

E

empathic, 13, 27, 45, 62, 65, 78, 88, 93, 98, 104, 105, 106, 118, 126, 130, 135, 136
empathy, 4, 27, 29, 30, 47, 57, 77, 96, 101, 105, 106, 118, 123, 127
emptiness, profound, 26
enforcer, 22
evil, 39, 45, 46, 47
exercise of power, 24

F

faith, 43, 44, 46, 47, 48, 51, 71
Farber, Leslie, 65, 148
fascist, 89
fear, 11, 15, 39, 44, 45, 46, 48, 49, 53, 79, 80, 82, 83, 84, 89, 122, 141
feels dishonest, 12
fight, 22, 88, 112, 123, 127
fluid boundaries, 7
Freud, Sigmund, 22, 99, 119, 148
frustrated, 1, 26, 122

G

"Go fight City Hall", 22
God, 40, 42, 43, 44, 45, 46, 47, 48, 49, 50, 51, 52, 98, 109, 137
Goffman, Erving, 13, 14, 148
good, 2, 7, 10, 14, 28, 45, 46, 47, 56, 71, 97, 102, 112, 120, 128, 134, 136, 140, 141, 142
grandiose, 23, 30
grossly negligent behavior, 5
guilt, 11, 12, 14, 15, 40

H

holding on, 122
homeostasis, 68, 113
honesty, 30
humanism, 88
hyperbolically, 66
hypnotism, 119

I

incipient panic, 9, 11, 126
indifference, 18, 19, 94, 97, 99, 115, 118
indignation, 10, 88
inference, 30, 54, 58, 61, 62, 85, 137, 146
informer, 2, 5, 6, 7
insolent manner, 18
interrelating, 12, 16, 20, 21, 69, 72, 94, 101, 106, 108, 126, 145
intervention, 37, 142, 145
intimacy, 2, 20, 26, 42, 43, 47, 52, 62, 73, 91, 92, 94, 101, 108, 135, 145, 146
intimidate, 29

J

Jehovah, 44
judge, 47
justification, 21, 24, 62, 102, 125

K

Knots, 91, 148
Kohutian, 62
Kristeva, Julia, 51

L

Laing, R.D., 91, 136, 148
Lash, Christopher, 53
libelous, actions, 15
lonesomeness, 52
loyalty, 49

M

madness, 67, 69
malingering, 36, 40, 130
mania, 31
manic depressive, 35, 36
manipulate, 30, 118, 145
market, 34, 142
master-slave relationship, 48
mediation, 41
mental health, 32, 131, 134, 137, 138, 139, 142
mindlessness, 23
mind-set, 36
moral superiority, 14
moralizing, 21

N

narcissism, 53, 102
narcissistic, 6, 14, 15, 30, 38, 50, 54, 60, 62, 64, 66, 72, 77, 88, 89, 93, 94, 96, 101, 104, 105, 113, 121, 123, 126, 127, 135
narcissistic injury, 6, 14, 15, 72, 77, 89, 104, 105, 121, 123, 126, 127
narcissists, 126
needs, 1, 17, 20, 21, 22, 34, 38, 40, 43, 49, 52, 54, 55, 63, 67, 68, 70, 72, 81, 89, 95, 101, 102, 104, 105, 114, 127, 128, 136, 137, 138, 140
negative closure, 63
New Testament, 44
Nixon defense, 16
nurturance, 27, 39, 60, 61, 62, 96

O

object relations, 20
objective evidence, 13
obsessionalism, 87
one-night stand, 21
one-upmanship, 53
other, 39, 110

P

pain, 25, 27, 28, 29, 30, 37, 38, 39, 40, 95, 97, 117, 123, 140
panic, 5, 9, 10, 78, 106
paradoxical, 79
paranoia, 14, 123
paranoid, 88, 113, 123, 126
passive, 88, 142
pastoral counselors, 40
pathological interaction, 16
payback, 122
pedagogic, 21
persona, 47, 58, 136
personality, 44, 68, 111, 120, 133, 136
personally humiliating, 4
Phillips, Adam, 42, 51, 78, 83, 115, 125, 148
philosophical, 42
ploy, 24, 60, 62, 91, 107
Portrait of the Artist as a Young Dog, 115, 148
Portrait of the Artist as a Young Patient, 34, 134, 147
posture of grandiosity, 14
power game, 7, 17, 30, 31, 35, 40, 53, 54, 70, 85, 86, 90, 93, 96, 101, 110, 111, 116, 119, 120, 136, 142, 146
Power Plays, 85, 101, 147
power transaction, 23
prayer, 40, 42
promiscuous, 82
pseudo intellectualism, 61
psychiatric ward, 35
psychic invalid, 36
psychic or real crime, 12
psychic pain, 39
psychically redundant, 96
psychological, 13, 38, 42, 47, 95, 119
psychotherapist, 19, 44, 58, 59, 86, 128
punishing and controlling, 6
punishment, 12, 44, 81

punitive, 13, 21, 45, 64, 88, 96, 97, 99, 123

R

radical premise, 20
radio relating, 31
recovery group, 36, 37
reductionism, 33, 57
rejection, 51, 64, 65, 87, 99, 104, 105
relational distance, 26
relationship, 6, 21, 24, 30, 33, 34, 37, 38, 39, 40, 42, 43, 44, 45, 46, 47, 48, 49, 50, 51, 52, 53, 55, 57, 62, 65, 66, 67, 69, 70, 71, 72, 77, 78, 82, 87, 88, 90, 91, 93, 94, 95, 113, 115, 124, 125, 126, 128, 129, 130, 131, 133, 142, 143, 145
reparation, 6, 14, 16, 38, 62
responsibility, 16, 26, 30, 40, 58, 60, 94, 95, 103, 107, 118, 135, 139, 140
rupture, 12

S

sadomasochistic, 88, 99
secondary defense, 15
seductiveness, 30
self, 1, 2, 7, 12, 14, 16, 17, 22, 26, 34, 35, 39, 42, 44, 46, 53, 54, 56, 59, 62, 63, 65, 66, 68, 69, 70, 71, 77, 78, 79, 80, 81, 84, 85, 91, 95, 96, 97, 98, 101, 102, 110, 111, 113, 118, 119, 120, 121, 123, 126, 127, 128, 134, 135, 136, 137, 139, 140, 141, 143
Self and Other, 136
shame and humiliation, 11
sin, 44, 45, 46
skills, 18, 102, 110
sociopathic, 16
solipsistic, world, 2
sound bites, 33
spontaneity, 20, 33, 43, 97, 145
stonewalling, 114

straight man, 118, 119, 120, 146
strategies, 103
Sullivan, Harry Stack, 88, 148
superego, 7, 22, 96, 97, 98, 99
surge of power, 23
symbiotic, union, 1, 123

T

tangential nurturing, 114
Terrors and Experts, 42, 83, 139, 148
The Dark Side of the Analytic Moon, 139, 147
the informer, 2
"The Theory of Games and Psychoanalysis", 147
theologians, 43
therapist, 5, 32, 42, 59, 133, 134, 135, 136, 137, 138, 139, 140, 141, 142, 143
therapy, 18, 35, 36, 37, 41, 53, 111, 133, 134, 138, 139, 142, 143, 146
Thomas, Dylan, 115, 148
threat, 6, 15, 40, 60, 79, 83, 93
tough love, 56
toxicity, 65
tragedy, 56, 117
transgressors, 12
traumatic, 11, 13, 14, 17, 39, 74, 77, 105
trivialization, 28, 57

U

ultimatum, 3
unacceptable impulses, 12
uncomfortable and guilty, 8
unconscious, 7, 12, 13, 16, 21, 23, 33, 34, 36, 39, 43, 44, 48, 52, 54, 56, 57, 62, 65, 67, 69, 78, 79, 82, 84, 93, 94, 99, 101, 103, 107, 108, 109, 115, 119, 120, 121, 122, 123, 125, 137, 138, 139, 140
unspeakable act, 11, 16

V

victimization, 123
voice of experience, 27

W

"waiting for Godot", 120

Winnicott, D.W., 141, 148
Wittgenstein, L., 115, 148
wrongfully accused, 7, 12, 16

Z

zero-sum, 1

www.ingramcontent.com/pod-product-compliance
Lightning Source LLC
Chambersburg PA
CBHW031553300426
44111CB00006BA/297